Ghosts of Upstate South Carolina

John Boyanoski

Shelor & Son Publishing, LLC

ISBN 13: 978-0-9761460-0-1
ISBN 10: 0-9761460-0-2

Library of Congress Control Number: 2006928509

Copyright © 2006 by Shelor & Son Publishing, LLC

Shelor & Son Publishing, LLC
312 Fairmount Terrace
Mountville, PA 17554

www.SHELORandSON.com

For Shonda and Hannah

Contents

Acknowledgments

I would like to thank my parents, Pete and Paula Boyanoski. Mom always rented scary movies on the weekends and let me watch them even though a couple scared me from going into the basement at night for several months. A fishing or hunting trip with Dad was never really complete unless he told a story about a haunted church, a ghostly hitchhiker, or some other spectral creature that loomed in the mountains where we lived.

I would also like to thank my great-aunt Julia O'Hop, whose tales of ghostly miners and haunted swamps first interested me in storytelling so many years ago.

My wife, Shonda, is due a world of credit for her support and patience.

Of course, my two sisters and brother, who tormented their younger sibling with ghost stories growing up, need to know they helped. My friend Mike Foley, who gave me a swift kick in the butt whenever I really felt like abandoning this project, is also due thanks.

And my publisher, Derik Shelor, who came up with the idea for this book in the first place.

The Man in Black in the Blue House
A Servant's Ghost Still Haunts a Spartanburg Home

Attorney Franklin Henson was working in his then-Alabama Street office one Saturday morning in the late 1980s when someone tapped at his first-floor window. A man and woman were standing outside and were asking if they could talk to him. They looked mild-mannered and harmless, so he walked out of his office into the main foyer and to the front door. The man introduced himself and said he had lived in the house in the 1960s while a college student. Henson and the man chatted for a few minutes, then the visitor asked a startling question.

"Have you seen the ghost?"

Henson looked back and answered no. He then added, "Is there a ghost?"

"Oh, yes," the man replied. "I saw it years ago."

"Well, tell me about it."

The visitor described seeing an apparition of an African-American man wearing long, black formal attire walk down the steps and go through the motions of opening the front door. The guest assumed the spirit was that of a former butler in the home. Henson smiled and assured him that he had never seen anything.

Now, Franklin Henson doesn't scare easily. As a pre-teen, he took a dare to sneak into Magnolia Cemetery not far from downtown during a snowstorm. His friends had told him a ghastly tale of a mausoleum that had been broken into and how a skeleton was laying in its coffin in plain view. He saw

1

the skeleton through a windowpane and made a fast exit. But he was able to compose himself enough later that day to call the authorities about the break-in. And now a respected attorney in Spartanburg, Henson certainly wasn't going to let the story of a ghost spook him.

But to be on the safe side, he didn't tell his staff because he didn't want them to get creeped out. A few months later, though, they would get their chance. That morning, as usual, Henson's secretary got to the office around 7:30 and locked all the doors behind her.

The Queen Anne-style building was constructed in 1899. It is a very impressive structure, with its gables and soft blue siding. By the time Henson was working there it had been converted into several offices on two floors. A wood-floored foyer separates the downstairs offices, and a large, ornate stairwell leading to the second story is the dominant feature of the room.

Tightly secured in her office, the secretary looked out into the foyer and saw an elderly black man wearing a dark black outfit standing at the bottom of the stairs. A little surprised, she got up to tell the man they weren't open yet, but by the time she got to the foyer the man was no longer there. She frantically checked the double front doors. They were locked tight.

Henson said she was a little agitated and even more confused by the time he arrived later that morning. She told him what she had seen, and he confessed to her about what the visitors had said several months before.

"We were both in amazement," he recalled. "After that I realized there was a ghost in there."

Henson said he never saw the visitor, but he often felt a cold spot while walking down the stairway. And sometimes he would talk to it late at night when no else was there.

"I know it sounds crazy, but once in a while I would just call out to let him know I was leaving or just to see how he was doing," Henson said.

Henson added that a friend of his told him the ghost of a young child who died in the kitchen also haunted the building.

2

Other people have reported seeing a young white woman looking out of an upstairs window.

Henson moved out after two years in the building, but he said it had nothing to do with ghosts. His story, though, serves as just the tip of the proverbial ghostly iceberg. The house changed hands several times over the next few years. Current building owner Mike Davis has dozens of strange tales from the building, of events that he hopes are things of the past.

Davis owns an advertising company, AD South, and moved it into the building in 1995. Not long afterward, he was working upstairs when he thought he heard a large throng of children running through the first floor. A father of five, he knows what a large group of excited kids sounds like, and he rushed downstairs to see who had come through. No one was there, and all the doors were closed. He would later hear the same noise coming from upstairs. He said it is indistinct, but the children are in a hurry. He can never make out what they are saying.

Things only got stranger. He sometimes heard someone or something walking up and down the main steps. The phones were another problem. A strange blowing sound came through, as if someone had picked up while he was talking. One of his employees got exasperated one day with the phone and asked Davis to get it fixed. The phone company checked the lines. There was no problem. It wasn't until a few months later that he started to get some answers as to what might be causing the sound. Of course, the explanation that it might be ghosts didn't make him feel any better.

A woman called up one day to see if Davis could do some radio ads for her. This was for a large Spartanburg company, and Davis told her where to find his office so she could drop off the information. As soon as he said the blue house on Alabama, the woman let out an exclamation.

"You're in the haunted house."

He was a little surprised that someone from a major company would say something so odd, but she soon explained. A previous owner—not Henson—had told her about the various disturbances in the house, and one time she had even seen a woman in turn-of-the-century clothing peering down at her from an upstairs room. Somehow the spirit had told the woman to stop the work being done on the house. The woman had then asked the owner if he was going to do any more renovations. He replied he was about tear out the old chimneys. She convinced the owner it wasn't the best idea to anger the spirit. Now loaded with some questions to ask, Davis decided to call up the previous owner, who confessed to having heard the mysterious children running through the house as well as seeing the black man that Henson's secretary had seen.

Davis felt it was odd, but he decided to keep the house. However, what happened next really tested his nerves. He was working upstairs editing some audio files. He had put very large headphones on when he heard what sounded like someone walking up the back porch steps. It was getting dark and cold, and he wondered if a homeless person had found his yard and was looking for a place to stay. He looked out the blinds, but no one was near the steps. He then checked the back door. No one was there either. Within ten seconds of hearing the sound, Davis was back in the audio room. He closed the door, but didn't shut it tight, and again put on the headphones. He turned his back to the door, but he then heard the door slowly creak open. He held his breath as he turned to see who had come in. No one was there.

"It was like something out of an Orson Welles horror movie," he said.

Needless to say, Davis went home, but the strange occurrences kept coming for him and his staff. He asked one of his graphic artists if he had ever noticed anything strange while working. Davis told him what had happened to him, and the man sort of let out a sigh of relief.

He could now tell Davis a story he had been reluctant to share before, fearing his boss would think he was a little crazy. The man said he was working one night and looked across the hallway and saw a woman standing in Davis's office. He assumed it was Davis's wife, Peggy, because the woman was looking at pictures behind the desk. He had then looked down, but then realized Peggy shouldn't have been in the building at the time. He looked back up and the apparition was gone.

Another day Davis arrived at work to find the police there. A secretary had come in early to get some work done and had locked the doors behind her. She hadn't been there very long before she heard something come tumbling down the stairwell. She thought it might be a burglar so she called the city police. There was no one there.

Davis then started to do some research on the house in the main county library. He found evidence of a fire at one time. Could that be the reason he hears children running in a commotion? However, he couldn't find much more that would explain what was causing the spirits.

The strange goings-on would affect him in other ways as well. One morning he came in to hear rushing water. There are no showers in the building, so he could only fear what the spirits might be up to this time. He was somewhat relieved when he found it was the hot water heater that had busted.

"At least that was something I could deal with," he said.

Another time, the police came to the house when it *was* burglarized. Someone had broken in overnight, but their robbery was strange. They took only a few things from an upstairs office, as if they knew the equipment they wanted. Yet they left numerous more expensive items there. And instead of leaving out the front or back doors, they escaped through an upstairs window. Had they heard or seen one of the ghosts and taken off in a hurry, thinking it was a living person? Or maybe they saw a ghost and knew exactly what it was.

One of Davis's children once offered a simple solution to figure out was going on. The company has numerous audio and visual devices, so why not let them run one night to see what could be seen? There is only one problem with that idea, Davis said. He isn't sure he wants to see what could be on the tapes.

5

Davis remains rational about what may be causing the disturbances, though. He thinks Einstein's theory that time and space can bend is a possible solution for what happens. Someone from the past is simply reliving their everyday experiences in the house. It could explain the phantom butler and the running children.

However, Davis eventually had enough of the rumblings. Around 2004, he simply called out one day for the spirits to leave. He told them this wasn't their time and place anymore. He said he doesn't believe in things like exorcisms, but it worked. He hasn't heard or seen a thing since.

The Ghosts of Old Abbeville
There Are Enough Stories Here to Scare Anyone

High up on the deserted second balcony of the Abbeville Opera House sits a lone, dust-covered chair. There are no other seats around for two whole rows. The chairs on the wings are connected to each other in a design similar to those seen in movie theaters. This is just a solitary chair.

And it's haunted.

Michael Genevie, the Opera House's executive director, said actors have told stories for generations of seeing a woman wearing turn-of-the-century clothing rise from her seat and start clapping during standing ovations. When they ask who was sitting alone in the third-floor balcony, they are always told the balcony has not been used in decades. And no one has a special pass to get up there during shows either.

Genevie has never seen the ghost (he first acted at the Opera House in 1978), but he admits that the story is part of the legend of haunted Abbeville and that it can't be taken lightly. Based on what I found researching this book, Abbeville would rival Charleston for the number of ghost stories per capita. There are numerous spooks in this town, but none is more famous than the woman in the Opera House. The theater started construction in the town square in 1900 and opened in 1908 to house touring New York shows that were heading to Atlanta. Over the decades, stars such as Jimmy Durante, Lesh Larue, and Tom Mix performed on the wooden stage inside the brick-facade building.

For much of its early years, the third-floor balcony where the ghost now resides was where African Americans watched shows. As segregation waned, the "colored-only" entrance and sitting area fell out of use. Sitting so high above the stage, you get a bit of a head rush looking down on to the main floor, and unfortunately it is no longer open to the public, Genevie said. But that's due to fire hazards rather than fear of a spectral ghoul. With only one entrance and exit, the fire marshal said it's unsafe for large crowds to gather up there.

However, no one can give an answer on who the mysterious woman might be. Was she a performer? A patron of the arts? Someone who died inside before the Opera House was completed? Does she have anything to do with a fatal shootout that occurred in 1910? Genevie said he has heard numerous legends, but none can be tied directly to the ghost.

And while the Opera House has one famed ghost story, the Belmont Inn, located just across the street, seems to have as many ghost stories as it does rooms. But Becky Holbert, the desk clerk since the mid-1990s, dismisses most of them with a laugh.

"The ghost stories grow every year with the wait staff," she joked.

Stories of a ghost named Abraham and of a Scotsman living on the main staircase Holbert gives a skeptical eye. But there are some things even this full-time schoolteacher can't explain so easily.

One of the hotel's owners was staying overnight and asked for a wake-up call at 6:30 A.M. However, a powerful storm came through and knocked out the electricty, and along with it the instructions for the morning desk clerk to place the call. But right on time the next morning, someone or something knocked on the man's door. As the owner was leaving that morning, he thanked the clerk on duty for the prompt knock. The desk clerk answered that he didn't send anyone to knock on the door. He didn't know it was supposed to be done.

Kitchen staff often have complained of plates, silverware, and the like flying off counters for no reason and of other items vanishing only to reappear a few hours later, she said. And a frantic guest once told Holbert that she looked in her mirror and saw a man with long hair standing in the doorway behind her.

"Now that's the stuff that makes you wonder," she said. "Those are good ghost stories."

The Peterson family bought the historic structure in 1996. Alan Peterson said he had seen and heard many of the strange tales, but can't confirm how many are true and how many are just the normal accidents attributable to the day-to-day operation of a hotel. He rattled off a long list of ghosts that have been reported to him over the years. He takes note of them, but doesn't let them scare him.

"It really doesn't bother me," he said.

With two well-known hauntings in tow, some in this Upstate community started to wonder what other legends might be lurking, said Cheri Standridge, executive director of the Abbeville Chamber of Commerce. When the Chamber solicited some stories a few years back with the help of the local newspaper, they got enough to create a two-hour ghost walk through most of downtown during the Halloween season.

Abbeville has a cozy little downtown situated around a rectangular "square." Numerous restaurants, coffee shops, antiques stores, and the like surround it. The town was where the first votes for secession from the Union occurred just prior to the Civil War. It is also the last place that Confederate president Jefferson Davis held a cabinet meeting while fleeing pursuing Union forces.

The highlights of the ghost tour include a house on Main Street where residents have said there is a rocking chair that moves on its own and never collects dust. Standridge said the family has tried numerous times to prevent the chair from rocking by putting weights on it, but the chair will still creak by itself. People there have also reported seeing dinner guests at a Christmas party mysteriously disappear from the table when they walk in. The family also reports hearing footsteps coming from the dining room when no one is there.

Ruth Freeman of the Abbewood Bed and Breakfast, located across town, tells a story about the renovation of the B&B in 1989. Her husband, Charlie, found what sounded like a hollow spot in one of the walls. Interested in what might be in there, they knocked down the wall and found a small set of three steps and a very old horsehair rug amid the cobwebs and dust. They cleaned up the area and, while thinking it a bit odd, didn't worry about the steps. But a few months later a man who grew up in the old house came by to see how the work was going. When he saw the steps, he remarked that they had let out the ghost of Mr. Norwood.

J.R. Norwood was a member of a very prominent Abbeville family in the 1800s. According to the visitor, he overheard his parents tell guests at dinner parties that Norwood had died on the steps and that his ghost was there. The steps were enclosed sometime in the late 1800s.

The Freemans wondered if Norwood's ghost was behind a strange odor coming from the dining room and the footsteps they sometimes heard in the upstairs bedrooms. They tried for more than a decade to get rid of the smell, but no combination of cleaners worked. They even called exterminators to see if something was decaying, but that didn't work either. It wasn't until a medium from Anderson County came to town that they got their answer. There was a ghost in the dining room, but it wasn't Norwood. It was not an evil ghost, but it was trying to hide something. The medium recommended lighting some sage to get the ghost to leave. Skeptical, Ruth bought a sage candle. The sound of footsteps upstairs can still be heard, but the smell in the dining room never came back.

Workers and visitors at the Abbeville Historical Society report hearing bootsteps on that building's stairs when no one is walking up them. And Standridge, herself, has had a bizarre personal experience inside the building. She was upstairs one December when someone from downstairs yelled that the light in the bathroom had gone out. After flipping the switch up and down a few times, they figured it was either a blown fuse or a burnt-out bulb. Another woman in the building went to fetch a light bulb because nobody wanted to hunt for the breaker box in the basement.

Returning with a new bulb, the woman flipped the switch out of habit as Standridge stood hovering with a flashlight. The light turned on immediately.

"You really can't explain it all," she said.

And you really can't explain all of the strange goings-on in Abbeville. Is it a large contingent of ghosts, or something else?

Poinsett Bridge
Historic Bridge Draws Its Share of Haunts

Joel Poinsett's influences on American life and more directly Greenville County are almost uncountable. A diplomat and scientist, he discovered the red, leafy plant that is a staple of the holiday season and bears his name. And he was the U.S. secretary of war under President Martin Van Buren. He was one of the prominent settlers of Greenville in the early part of the nineteenth century. But for lovers of ghost stories, Poinsett's name is most notably linked to a bridge that is the site of several hauntings.

Poinsett designed and built the 130-foot-long bridge that spans Little Gap Creek in 1820. Photographs of its fourteen-foot-high arch are often seen on postcards and tourist guides to Greenville. Located in the far northern edge of Greenville County, the bridge has been the object of numerous restoration efforts and is no longer open to vehicular traffic. But that doesn't stop people from trying to drive up there to take pictures, eat a picnic, or look for the ghosts that are so attached to the structure.

According to one legend, a slave was once hung under Poinsett Bridge and his ghost still haunts it. Several of the locals say that they have been unable to start their cars when they got ready to leave. A light is said to move toward them as they sit slack-jawed in their vehicles. Several locals also report that they hear a loud scream when the light gets to them.

Another variation of the tale is that there is an Indian burial ground nearby and that at midnight their souls arise, which causes the cars to knock out and screams to be heard. Another legend states the souls of the men who died building the bridge haunt it. It should be noted that the ghosts are usually referred to as being those of Chinese immigrant workers, but there is no evidence that anyone of Chinese descent helped build the bridge.

The strange tales surrounding the old bridge have drawn numerous visitors, including North Carolina-based paranormal investigator Patrick Burleson, who has tried several times to find what may be lurking at the bridge and in the densely forested surrounding areas. Burleson admits his first several stabs at finding ghostly evidence were unsuccessful, but that was because he and his team had trouble finding the bridge. It is very remote, after all. His crew finally found the bridge on Halloween night 2003 after combing the mountains in the area.

"We split into two groups, and one of the groups started hollering that they had found the bridge, so we had to run down the mountain to get to them," he recalled.

His crew set up infrared cameras and electronic monitors around 1 A.M. in hopes of catching a glimpse of something in the wilderness or along the bridge. The cameras can pick up objects that are invisible to the naked eye, while the monitors can pick up shifts in electronic vibrations. Most often, a strong reading on the meter will usually lead to something being caught on camera that can't be explained, he said.

The first of these is "ecto," which is the mist form of a spirit, Burleson said. It is often seen in a gray, foggish color, but is too well defined to be mist from a cigarette or actual fog. The second is "orbs," which are small spheres of light that sometimes accompany ecto or can be seen on their own.

"We can't say what they are," he said. "That's the whole reason we do this. We want to know what these really are and how they play into ghost legends."

After taking several rolls that night, his crew went home to develop the film. There wasn't much until they got to the fifth

13

picture and found what appeared to be ecto. The find was somewhat akin to an NFL fan finally getting tickets to the Super Bowl. That glimpse was enough to convince Burleson and his team to return to the Poinsett Bridge in 2004.

On Halloween 2004, they made the four-hour drive to the bridge in northern Greenville. There was no rain—unlike in 2003—but this time a lot of novice ghost hunters also came to the bridge, separate from Burleson's team. His group was happy to share information about the bridge with them, but with that many people around it was tough to get good pictures.

Keeping their investigation low-key was hindered by the additional people. Even though the location is desolate and remote, sheriff's deputies still patrol the area. So, every time a car's headlights cut through the night, people scattered into the surrounding underbrush.

One of the people who scattered was a member of Burleson's group, Adam. After he didn't return in a few minutes, they started calling his name. He popped up saying he had gotten lost in the woods, but Burleson noted that his associate looked upset. Adam disappeared again when another vehicle was seen coming, and again he did not return. Burleson said that he and another member of the team decided to walk the old roadway that crosses the bridge to get a better picture of it. The legends state most of the activity is in the bridge's center. They soon heard something behind them in the trees.

"The next thing we know, here comes Adam walking out of the woods—not running, but really fast. He stops in front of us, looks directly at us, and says, 'There's something in the woods,' and then keeps walking for the bridge," Burleson said.

Burleson said they ran after Adam, and when they shined their flashlights on his arms there were scratches and bruises all over them. They looked like little cuts and scratches from an animal. Adam said he didn't remember getting them, but he may have fallen in some briars. Or maybe something else happened?

"He was just really spooked," Burleson said.

Adam then told the story of what had occurred during those few minutes in the woods. When the car drove by, he took off and quickly got lost in the pitch-black forest. After a few minutes he came to a clearing where some moonlight fell. He walked up to it and saw two "orbs" floating in the sky a few feet from the ground. One was red. The other was blue. Adam said he felt fear freeze over him. He was unable to move his legs to run away. His voice couldn't cry out for help. All he could do was stare helplessly at the floating balls of lights.

Then all of a sudden he worked up the gumption to turn and run into the woods. With no way of knowing if he was going in the right direction, he ran, walked, and crawled through the undergrowth and past towering trees with the dread thought that something was following him very closely. But every time he turned around, he could not see anything. Exhausted, he reached the road and saw his friends. He wasn't able to run, but walked as fast as he could back to the car.

After the strange encounter in the woods, the rest of the group set up a Ouija board near the bridge to see if that might lead to some answers. Burleson said a lot of paranormal investigators debunk the use of the boards. On one end of the spectrum, some see the boards as being unreliable, but another group of investigators said the boards are too powerful to be used in the open.

Burleson said he must fall in the middle, because every time his group has used a board it was able to pick up something that correlated with the oddities seen in pictures taken.

However, at the bridge in 2004, the board's planchette went back and forth with little rhyme or reason and the investigators were unable to interpret anything. The group's pictures showed enough that he plans to make more trips to investigate Poinsett Bridge.

"It was something that we want to keep looking into," Burleson said. "For us, it is probably the biggest haunting in the region. It's something that can't be explained, but I guess that is what we want to do."

A Ghostly Love Story
Some Strange Tales from Newberry College

Newberry College's beautiful campus is located in the tiny, historic town of the same name. And like many other campuses in the Upstate, it has a ghost story, one that dates back generations. Gordon Henry, a college and county historian, said the main legend involves a Southern belle, a Union solider garrisoned at Newberry College after the war, and a tale of love lost in the 1860s.

The school had started as a Lutheran seminary decades before, but much of the seminary had moved to a campus in Lexington in 1831. By 1855, there were few students left on campus, so the General Assembly decided to grant the school a charter as a degree-granting college, Henry said. Ten years later, the small campus became an ideal spot to station Union cavalry troops in the turbulent months after the war. It was also a place for a love story to blossom.

A young woman named Madeline fell in love with one of the Bluecoats, Henry said. According to a story by Dr. Thomas Epting in the school magazine, it was love at first sight for both. However, it was not meant to be, as the young soldier was transferred to a faraway post and subsequently died in the service. A downtrodden Madeline was inconsolable and often visited the campus to remember her few days with the soldier. Her morose feelings eventually got the better of her and she climbed the highest tower, Keller Hall, and taking a step forward plunged herself into death.

According to the Epting legend, her death occurred on November 17, which was the anniversary of their meeting. Since that time, Madeline's wayward ghost is said to return to the campus every year seeking the young man who got away. Her moans and sobs can be heard near Keller Hall. Students claim the young girl's scream still pierces the late November night, reliving her fatal plunge. Some have actually claimed to have seen the young woman watching them from high above.

Another version of the story revolves around Madeline, but this time her lover is named John, and he may or may not be a Union soldier. This legend states John was killed in a horse and buggy race in the 1860s. The death of her loved one apparently triggered an emotional collapse and she ended up in a mental hospital. She was unable to believe that John was dead, so the hospital staff let her return every November 17 to search for him among the buildings. The search, of course, never turned up anything, but the hospital staff let her return year after year. She eventually convinced the orderlies to let her search atop Keller Hall. From there, Madeline took her fatal plunge.

However, a third story exists, and this time it is John who takes the fall. Madeline and John were planning to get married as soon as he finished his studies at the college, which was an all-men's school at the time. He learned that his beloved Madeline was stepping out, as they say, with other men around Newberry. An angry John couldn't believe what he had heard and took a long walk on a cold November night. In a fit of despair, he climbed the steps of Keller Hall and stared across the evening sky. The view was not enough to curb his anxieties about Madeline's alleged dalliances. He then leapt to his death and landed in a bloody, twisted heap at the base of the building.

At just about the same time, Madeline went to the campus to tell John she had been unfaithful. Carrying a small lantern to light her way, she found the young man's body and realized her treachery had led to his death. It is said she released a scream that could be heard all over Newberry County.

Henry said students recreated the story of Madeline and John for decades every November. Someone would invariably wear a black cloak that covered their face and body as they carried a lantern around campus as part of the show. Sometimes a student would dress all in white and climb Keller Hall. Those reenactments ended in the 1960s, but the ghost story still circulates among students.

However, Henry said he has some reservations about the story.

"There has never ever been any proof found that any of the stories ever occurred," he said. "And if they did happen, it's odd that they chose Keller Hall."

The reason, Henry said with a chuckle, is that Keller Hall wasn't built until 1895. That is a heck of a long time for a young woman scorned by her lover in the 1860s to wait to jump from a building. However, Keller Hall does have a rather morbid, but curious history.

The Victorian-style building is the only one on campus named after a student, James Aiken Keller, who died of typhoid fever during his sophomore year in 1884. His mother, Frances E. Keller, provided funds to help construct the building the next year in honor of her beloved son. Despite the tragic story that led to the building's start, the ghost of young James Keller has never been reported. Over the years, the building served as a chapel, library, science hall, and auditorium. Those duties were moved to other facilities over the decades, and by the 1980s it had fallen out of use. The building was placed on the National Register of Historic Places in 1976, and as of 2006 there are efforts to get it restored.

Keller is also the home of the school's second most famous mystery, after the ghost story, of course. When the college went north to Walhalla for about a decade after the Civil War, the school's original bell went along for the trip. It was believed that it returned to the campus as the bell in the tower of Keller Hall. That proved false when the college decided to remove the

Keller Hall bell in the 1980s for structural purposes. The bell in the tower was cast in the 1890s in Baltimore.

So, what happened to the school's original bell? No one really knows.

A second ghost legend on campus revolves around Kinard Hall, a two-story, 1960s-style, brick building. Henry said he was not aware of the story, but students have reported water faucets turning on by themselves, cabinets and drawers suddenly opening on their own, and windows in some rooms opening of their own volition. All of the legends are associated with the building's second floor.

The Many Ghosts of Converse College
Hauntings Abound on Spartanburg Campus

Converse College, with its decades-old gothic buildings, lush green canopy of trees, and seclusion in downtown Spartanburg, is one of the most beautiful campuses in all of South Carolina. And easily one of the most haunted. For some reason this all-women's college is steeped in ghost stories. A former department head that still wanders the campus? Got one. A mysterious murder legend? Chalk that up. Tales of dead students and college employees still haunting the dorms? Oh yeah.

The stories have become part of the school's lore despite the best efforts of college officials to downplay them as simple tales meant to scare first-year students. Yet, they are as much a part of new students' introduction to campus life as becoming a Pink Panther or a Red Devil.

Converse's most famous ghost comes from what is likely the school's best-known educational field, music. The Petrie School of Music draws hundreds of applications a year from aspiring musicians. Its history dates back almost to Converse's 1889 founding.

One of the best-known professors in the school's history was Hazel B. Abbott, a drama teacher and the department head in the school of music from 1927 to 1956. The Hazel B. Abbott Theater, located on the third floor of stately Wilson Hall, is one of several theaters on campus. It focuses on smaller productions. Abbott's legacy at Converse is well deserved, but her name has become somewhat immortal due to the ghost legend surrounding her. Students have said the eyes in a painting of Abbott follow people, that she can be seen walking the catwalks during shows, and that people who sit in her chair will feel a cold presence.

I went to the theater to find out more about the legend. A large portrait of Abbott—the one whose eyes supposedly move—hangs in the lobby alongside replica Greek sculptures. Wearing a black dress adorned with white trim, she had a faint smile on her lips, but I did not see her eyes move. Several theater students nearby said they had heard upperclassmen swear to have seen Abbott's eyes move, but none of those present would vouch that they saw it themselves. Such is the problem with Converse's ghosts—many have heard of them, few have seen them.

But what about inside the theater? Like thousands of students over the decades, I entered through the white double doors. When alone in the theater, one does feel a bit cold and nervous—especially if the lights are out.

However, professor John Bald, whose office is one floor above the theater, said the ghost may be more student imagination than anything else. He has been at the college since the early 1980s and has not seen or heard anything except stories from students. Plus, the supposed chair that Abbott sat in has long since been removed as part of a major renovation to the music hall.

"She wouldn't even recognize the place," he said.

The students I talked to that day outside the Abbott Theater also let me in on another ghost in Wilson Hall. (The students didn't want to be named because Converse officials try to downplay this legend as well.) This ghost is in the stairway to the bell tower, the most visible landmark on the campus. Legend has it that two men were arguing up there and one was pushed off. It is said his ghost still haunts the bell tower. The event supposedly occurred in the 1920s, but the men's names and what they were arguing about has been lost to time. He is an angry ghost, rumored to have glowing red eyes. The stairwell to the bell tower is locked after the third-floor landing, so it remains to be seen what the students have found lurking in the shadows of Wilson. School officials, for the record, deny the background story to the ghost, and I couldn't find any outside corroboration of a murder. But students seem pretty convinced the story is true.

Connected to Wilson is Pell Hall, which is mostly a dormitory for seniors. There are numerous legends attached to Pell, including that of Mary G., a dorm mother whose ghost supposedly roams the first floor. Mary G., said to be a friendly ghost, has been known to make beds for students and tidy up around the building, students said. Who could ask for a better ghost?

Other legends passed along are the morbid tales of a student who hanged herself in the 1950s and another who fell from her window while trying to elope. Their ghosts haunt Pell as well, according to lore. Again, the stories behind these ghosts are shadowed in murky legend. The student who was said to have hanged herself strung a noose from the door in her room. Her name and why she chose such a ghastly way to end her life are open to debate among students. The door has been repainted and replaced numerous times, but no matter what, you can still see the outline of the rope, noose, and body. According to legend, she is a fairly hostile ghost. She has locked people in her room before. However, it seems that which room belonged to the girl changes from year to year, based on who the Converse students want to frighten.

While Wilson and Pell Halls' ancient brick facades date back to the school's founding, at least one newer dorm, Williams, also has a legend to it. Williams is a three-story, 1960s-style dorm on the edge of campus. It is said there is a ghost in the laundry room, a little boy who used to live there when Converse was a boarding school. He appears to be less than ten years old and is considered to be very friendly, though he doesn't do anything more than be seen standing in the room and then vanish into thin air before students can get a good look.

One former student said she and some friends spent a few weeks looking into the stories in the mid-1990s. They spent a lot of time with Ouija boards and the like, but never found anything. They kept looking for the grave of another young boy, whose mother's spirit was haunting the school's dining hall. They even went to the school library to look up some of the legends, but the stories they found were just speculative pieces passed on by other students through the decades. However, they did have one very strange encounter during their search.

One day, my source said, one of her friends was walking down the steps to the dining hall and loudly said she felt their whole search for the little boy was a waste of time. No sooner had the words left her mouth than she felt like she was pushed. She stumbled down the steps, but luckily was uninjured. The young woman was quickly admonished by her friends for having riled the ghost. The friend never joked about the ghost story again, but luckily never felt its presence again, either.

Ghost Road
Drive Down Old Piedmont Highway If You Dare

Driving down the long stretch of Old Piedmont Highway just south of Interstate 85 during daylight hours, you would have no reason to think anything was amiss. But if you drove the stretch of road late at night, you might soon find out why some call the highway Ghost Road.

Dave Sanders grew up in Greenville and said driving Ghost Road was a favorite pastime of teens around Halloween. Two popular stories about the stretch of road feature sad tales of someone who died too early. Their ghosts still haunt the area. One involves a man who was hit by a train barreling down one of the railroad tracks that run on both sides of the road. The other concerns a car that flipped while negotiating a curve in the fog, killing the driver. Both men are rumored to still roam the road at night. Unfortunately for Sanders, in 1983 he got to experience one of the ghost stories all too well, though he is still not quite sure which one it was.

Sanders and his friends hopped into his truck one Friday and headed toward Ghost Road around midnight. They passed an old graveyard and a couple of small houses. The pine trees on both sides of the road gave the appearance of driving down a dark tunnel with no end in sight. The road was almost pitch black when they noticed an eerie fog start to surround them. That spooked them enough to stop the truck and try to calm themselves. One of the friends said he had heard earlier on the radio that there was supposed to be fog that night. But no one wanted to listen to him, Sanders recalled. They were sure something was about to happen. The fog, whether supernatural or not, was a sign for them.

They started to drive again, the two yellow beams of their headlights barely cutting through the enveloping gray mist. What happened next scared Sanders for years to come.

Off to the left side of the road a small light appeared. It was about twenty-five yards away and the size of a baseball. The light seemed to be moving down the railroad tracks. Sanders's heart started to beat rapidly. His friends grew quiet as they peeked out the windows of his old Dodge. They started to slow down. When the truck stopped, the light stopped as well.

For a few seconds the light just stood there in the field. Sanders was hoping it was maybe a local landowner holding a flashlight or maybe some more teens playing a prank. But he knew what a flashlight or lantern looked like when being held. A lantern would sway ever so slightly. A flashlight would put off a beam of light. This wasn't doing either.

The light then flicked out for a second. But almost as soon as it had gone out it reappeared less than ten yards from the side of the truck. Sanders watched, his eyes fixed on the light. It was almost three feet off the ground and oddly shaped. It appeared somewhat round, but seemed to change shape every few seconds. Sanders's foot let go of the brake and slammed down on the accelerator.

He glanced over his left shoulder and could see the light steadily keeping pace with the truck. His friends encouraged him to go faster, but no sooner had they said that than the light flicked out again. Sanders kept going. He didn't bother to look over his shoulder to see if it was glowing again.

The friends found their way back to a main road in silence. None wanted to talk about what they had just seen. Sanders eventually broke the silence by saying it was probably someone with a flashlight and made a vain attempt to laugh. But how did the light keep up with them? It was someone on an ATV, Sanders thought quickly. That would explain the speed.

But why didn't they hear a motor out there? Sanders said he felt a chill when they said that. It had been completely silent. And why would the light change shape? None of them had an answer for that one.

Had they seen one of the fabled lights along Ghost Road? After that day, Sanders was convinced. The legend told among teens was that the car wreck was due to the dark road. The ghost of the driver returns with a light to warn drivers about the danger there. Sanders said that while the incident with the light scared him "nearly to death," he still drives the road once in a while looking for a glimpse of the ghost.

The Woman in the Window
A Ghost Story for Pickens

Unlike a lot of Upstate ghost legends—in fact most ghost legends—the little town of Pickens has a story whose history can easily be traced. But before getting to the story of Sarah McDaniel, one must understand a little about Pickens.

Named for a Revolutionary War hero, the Pickens County seat is a town at the crossroads. Neighboring Easley to the east is slowly surpassing it in terms of population and money, and Clemson to its southwest will forever be linked with its university and its Tigers football team. But the three thousand or so Pickens city residents share a common belief that their hometown is the best in South Carolina and one with a lot of history.

That history includes the benevolent ghost of Sarah McDaniel, who, it is said, haunts the Pickens County Museum, reports Allen Coleman, the museum's director. Coleman notes "said" because in all his years working at the museum he has never seen the apparition that supposedly looks forlornly out the windows at night.

But Grant Larkin says he saw it—or at least something—one frightful night a few decades ago. He and his friends had heard legends about the building and drove out there once in the early 1970s while they were all high school students in Anderson County.

"It was pretty spooky," he said. "I'm not sure how much of it was nerves and how much was something else."

27

The story of the ghost is an old one that has been passed around for decades. The museum was once the county jail, and Sarah McDaniel was the wife of James Henry Grace McDaniel, the first Pickens sheriff to live in the building off what is now U.S. Highway 178. Not long after moving there with their thirteen children in 1903, sewage backed into the well water. Five family members got typhoid fever, and Sarah McDaniel died in an upstairs apartment, which is now a gallery.

"The story goes Sarah always watched over her children," Coleman said. "She was so devastated over leaving them that she wouldn't leave."

To this day, people report seeing a woman looking out the window on dark nights when no one is supposed to be inside. The apparition is usually seen as a woman in white and is gone before the witness can get a good second look. One popular part of the legend is that McDaniel haunts the semi-circular tower on the right side of the building, overlooking the new jail, and that you can see her in the second-story window usually after 11:00 P.M. and most often during a full moon.

That is the part of the legend that Larkin remembered the most. He and his friends made the left off of 178 one Saturday night right before Halloween. They had tried to coordinate their effort with a full moon, but it was covered that night by a heavy blanket of clouds. They weren't sure if the full moon was up there or if it had passed the night before.

"We wanted to go the night before, but it was a school night," he said with a sigh years later.

Despite its being just off the road, Larkin said he and his friends passed by the building a couple of times without seeing it. They eventually got out of their car and grabbed a flashlight out of the trunk to cut through the dark night. It only took a few seconds before they saw the museum's distinctive front steps and the semi-circular tower rising over the small front yard.

The beam of Larkin's flashlight made its way up the side of the building, and he remembered stopping the beam right below the window for just a second. He felt his hand tremble, but he pushed the little yellow beam up just another foot skyward.

"There was something there in the window plainly outlined by my light," he said. "It had an almost whitish glow."

Before he could say anything, whatever he had seen was gone. He turned to one of his friends, and his flashlight's beam turned to his pal's face, which was mouth agape and eyes wide.

"Did you see it, too?" Larkin asked.

His friend just nodded up and down very slowly. The two others with them asked what was going on. They apparently had been looking the other way. And, of course, they were incredulous about the tale Larkin told. They thought it was a joke, but Larkin still remembers it as plain as day.

"I tried to rationalize it a couple of times," he said. "It was probably just my light refracting off something in the room. They may have had an old mirror up there or something."

Larkin added that he wasn't really all that scared by the experience, just curious. Meanwhile, Coleman, who has never seen the vision of McDaniel, said he has felt uneasy working there at night. Papers will go missing, only to turn up an hour later.

"I've had some interesting experiences, but I just chalk those up to being tired," he said.

Allen Coleman could not say how long the legend of Sarah McDaniel has been around. He first heard about it when he started working at the museum in the mid-1990s. There are no other ghosts associated with the old building on Johnson Street, despite its having been a jail for the first seventy years of its existence. And that is fine with Coleman. The legend of one ghost—even a benevolent one—is enough.

Little Leila
A Sad Tale of a Little Girl in Piedmont

The lone gravestone on the side of Highway 20 is barely noticeable to the drivers speeding down the curvy road in eastern Greenville County. But some who manage to turn their head in time claim to see the spirit of a little girl who died close to 150 years ago.

Leila Howell died on March 20, 1859, according to the Piedmont gravestone. She had recently turned three years old. According to the four-foot-high marker, she was the daughter of Dr. W.S. and S.C. Howell, and part of a prominent Piedmont family.

Piedmont is a unique town to the Upstate because of its massive size. It spans two counties and seems to stretch in all directions, from Interstate 85 in the north to Highway 20 in the south. However, the town center is located on the shoals of the Saluda River. There sit the remains of the town's old mill and the scattered mill village. Little Leila's grave site is several miles north of this popular fishing area.

M. Paul Rampey has lived in a home near the grave for more than fifty years and has gotten to know a lot about the legend of "Little Leila." The youngster apparently died of typhoid fever and was buried under an old oak tree where she often played on her parents' farm. The Howells eventually moved, and part of their land became the current Piedmont Highway that runs from downtown Greenville, crosses the Saluda River, and heads into Anderson County.

Unfortunately, Little Leila has not had a lot of rest over the years. Her grave has been struck numerous times over the decades, Rampey said. The number was too high for him to recall. The gravestone would never collapse, but it was bruised and battered beyond belief. The state Transportation Department eventually took control of the grave's upkeep and built the black wrought-iron fence around it that softens the blows of some of the accidents.

But what has caused all the accidents? The grave is relatively far off the road, and the curve is not that sharp. Can there be something attracting them to the grave?

Upstate paranormal investigator Harrison Setzler said the figure of a little girl dressed in white has been spotted playing alongside the highway at night and usually over the roadside grave. Others have claimed to have seen a small white orb hovering over the grave, he said. According to Setzler, there is a lot of unexplained energy at this sight, which to him means there is a spirit that could find rest.

Dave Sanders said he and his friends spent a lot of time as teens driving up and down the road looking for Little Leila in the 1980s, and while they had some other unexplainable encounters along the highway, they never saw any sign of the little girl.

"It's a sad tale, really," he said.

One man I found, however, said he saw something there once, but he wasn't quite sure what it was. Bill Ellington said he was coming from work one night in the early 1990s. It was a little after midnight, and he knew the road so well from driving it that he said he would kind of go on autopilot.

"I was probably speeding because I never saw anyone on the road at night," he said. "And then out of the corner of my eye I saw something flash. I knew it couldn't have been headlights. It was just a soft, white glow on the side of the road."

Ellington said he slammed on the brakes of his old pickup truck and sort of skidded to a halt. His body flung forward he stopped so fast. But by the time he turned around to see if the glow was still there, it had vanished. He believes he saw something, but he never heard the tale of Little Leila until years later, when he looked it up on a website.

"I'm convinced that is what I saw," he said.

Rampey, though, dismisses the tales, saying he's never seen anything but the gravestone of a young girl who died a tragic death and that speeding vehicles have given her no peace in the afterlife.

The Gaffney Strangler
A Grim Story of a 1960s Serial Killer

More than thirty years after their deaths, do the victims of the Gaffney Strangler still cry out for help along the deserted roads and creeks where he tossed their bodies all those decades ago?

For nine days in February 1968, the little town of Gaffney was terrorized by the thought that a serial killer was walking among them. Located a few miles from Interstate 95, Gaffney is a booming town now feeding off growth of Spartanburg to the west and Charlotte to the east, but back then a little less than nine thousand people lived there. It was a county seat, but still a very close-knit community surrounded by farms and pastures. It was not prepared for what happened. Practically every person in the town was scared of when and where the killer would strike next, according to newspapers at the time. Children were taken from schools by worried parents. Pawn shops sold out of handguns. Door-to-door salesmen didn't dare knock.

Everyone was unnerved except just one man—the killer himself, Lee Roy Martin, a textile worker and father of three small children. He killed four women ranging in ages from fourteen to thirty-two over a nine-month period. Not just killed, but strangled with a belt. After his arrest, he was all too eager to show a deputy how he did it. And decades after the brutal killings, people still talk about the women and tell of hearing their voices calling for help from beyond the grave. But that is getting ahead of the story.

The terror started on February 8, when a man called the local newspaper to give the detailed locations of the whereabouts of three victims. He ordered the reporter to call the Cherokee County Sheriff's Office and have them investigate. The reporter did so, but according to later accounts of the investigation, none of the deputies thought it was a real case.

That is, until they went to the bridge over the creek on Old Ford Road and saw the body of a naked woman with her head submerged in the muddy waters below. A bluish circular mark was around her neck. Deputies quickly went to the second location the caller had given, along Chain Gang Road, and to their horror they found the second victim's foot sticking out of some dead winter leaves.

Using the names given by the caller, police quickly realized one of the victims was a fourteen-year-old girl who had gone missing a week before while walking to see her mother in order to show off a new outfit. The other was a twenty-year-old woman who had been reported missing the night before while walking her new poodle.

But no sooner had the case gotten terrifyingly real, than it took an unexpected turn. The deputies went to the third location on Jerusalem Road, just a few hundred yards across the county line in neighboring Union County, but they couldn't find a dead woman. At least not that day. Union police quickly informed the investigators that they had found a naked woman strangled to death near a fence. But that had been the previous May. And they had already made an arrest. In fact, that man had already been convicted of the killing and was serving eighteen years in prison.

Confused momentarily, investigators got a break in the case when a man called in to say he had seen a late 1950s black Chevrolet along Old Ford Road on February 7. A man had gotten out of the car and had appeared to dump something into the river. Investigators now had a strong clue of what they were looking for, but many questions would remain unanswered until February 12.

That night the mysterious caller who had informed the reporter about the bodies phoned the newsman at home and gave chilling recounts of the murders and where to find the victims' belongings. He said he had called because he felt guilty that another man was serving his prison sentence for the 1967 murder. When the reporter asked the man why he didn't give himself up, the caller replied he didn't want to be killed by the police. Then the phone line clicked off. The reporter called the deputies, who soon arrived to ask questions. No sooner had they arrived than the phone rang again. The killer called to offer some bits of info and to warn that he would strike again unless the police arrested him soon.

Unfortunately for the residents of Gaffney, the strangler didn't give the police much time. The next morning, a fourteen-year-old honor student was waiting for the bus just a few hundred feet from her home. She usually waited with her sister, but this day she had gotten to the stop two minutes early. As her sister approached the stop, she saw a black car pull up and a man get out. He started to wrestle with the young teen, struggling with her as she fought back, and then he threw her in the trunk, slamming the metal door down over her. The sister walking up the driveway screamed for help, but it was too late. Her sister was the next victim of the Gaffney Strangler.

The entire community went into a panic as parents pulled their children from schools and businesses shut down in fear. One report said local pawn shops ran out of handguns as concerned husbands and fathers bought every last weapon they could find. Many cars went searching for the suspect's vehicle, which police were describing as a 1957 black Chevrolet. Two Gaffney men soon saw the car parked down an old dirt road. Convinced they had found the killer, they sped after the vehicle when the driver took off in a cloud of dust, but they could not catch up.

However, they were able to get a license plate number off the car and called the police. The tag was soon traced to Lee Roy Martin, a former taxicab driver and now a first shift textile

35

worker. With a slight build and short, dark hair, he was a rather modest-looking man. Deputies immediately began staking out Martin at work and at home. They saw him wash a black 1957 Chevrolet in his yard and clean off what appeared to be a bloody handprint from one of the windows. They also noticed that he never opened the trunk. They even learned that he had visited the homes of two of his victims in the days after the killings to offer condolences.

The Gaffney murders were now attracting a national audience—it had only been a few years since the Boston Strangler terrorized that city, and the Zodiac killer was then taunting California law enforcement that he could not be stopped. CBS sent a young reporter named Dan Rather to cover the search and fear in the little South Carolina town. One can only imagine the terror that swept Gaffney, heightened by the cold weather, desolate winter landscape, and mistrust of almost everyone they met.

On February 16, nine days after the first phone call, law enforcement officers arrested Martin as he left work. A woman nearby fainted when she found out why Martin was being arrested. When revived, she told deputies Martin had offered to escort her home because she was scared of the strangler.

With Martin's arrest, the man convicted of killing the woman in Union County was let go. Martin then led deputies on a tour of the eight spots spread out through the two counties where he had dumped bodies and belongings of the victims. During one of the trips, a deputy asked Martin how he had overpowered the women so easily. Martin offered to show the deputy and asked for a belt. The deputy thought nothing of it and handed over a belt. Within an instant, Martin had the belt around the man's neck and then interlocked his arms behind his back in a submission hold. The deputy was completely powerless. Martin would not stop the choking despite repeated orders to do so. It took several deputies to get him off the man. Martin then apologized, saying he got possessed when he had someone in his grip.

Martin was quickly convicted of the four killings and given life sentences in prison. His only explanation was that a split personality would take him over and kill the women. He had been able to control the second personality for years, but it was now getting too strong. Martin was subsequently stabbed to death in a state prison in Columbia in May 1972. His killer took his own life five years later.

But that is not the end of the twisted story. The state sold Martin's 1957 Chevrolet at an auction. According to newspaper accounts a few years later, the first man to own the car used to keep it parked in his driveway, and it often attracted visitors. Young women would ask the man to go for a drive in it. The excited young women would beg him to take them to the spots where the bodies had been dumped. Once there, many of the young women would freak out and run screaming from the car. They said they could hear sounds coming from the trunk. Women crying and someone scratching. The man said he had trouble getting some of the hysterical young women back home because they would not get back in the car.

The man subsequently sold the car to a collector, who spent a great deal of money restoring the vehicle back to its original condition. On the new owner's first drive in the refurbished car, he wrecked it. After that, the car's history is not known.

And now, almost forty years later, people in Gaffney say that if you drive by the overpasses, ditches, and creeks where Martin left the bodies you can still hear their moans.

However, not everyone is so sure of what happened with the ghost stories. Bill R. Gibbons wrote one of the definitive books about Martin, but he doesn't believe the haunted tales. He believes many of the stories of shrieking women and haunted cars were leftovers of the paranoia that gripped the community in 1968. He noted that he hasn't heard any new versions of the ghost stories in decades. Most of the tales originated just after Martin's arrest.

"We had some people look into the reports, and we could never find anything," he said. "I think it was kids and maybe even some adults letting their imaginations get away from them."

Or was it something else? The spirits of those killed, seeking justice from beyond the grave?

Ten Ghosts at the Merridun Inn
A Very Haunted Union County Story

The quiet Georgian-style Merridun Inn just outside of down-town Union is never short on guests, but that doesn't neces-sarily have to do with owner Peggy Waller's hospitality and reputation as a high-quality businesswoman. No, the small, five-bedroom Merridun has ten full-time ghosts that roam the hallways and grounds day and night. That bevy of spirits includes former owners, a caretaker, two as yet unidentified young children, two Cherokee Indians, and a dog. Despite the cramped space, all ten ghosts are very friendly and each seems to have a job to do around the bed and breakfast, whether it be tending to children, guiding travelers, or watching over Waller herself. And they find time for fun once in a while, such as a semi-annual Christmas party the ghosts hold in the main liv-ing room that can be heard over the hotel's intercom system during the night.

"It's kind of an interesting endeavor," Waller said. "They have made themselves very known over the years."

The hotel was originally built in 1855 by William Keenan, a former mayor of Union. Listed on the National Register of Historic Places, it is located on nine acres and surrounded by century-old magnolia trees. The Rice family bought it in 1876 and kept it in their family for seven generations. It picked up its somewhat unusual name from a conglomeration of Merriman, Rice, and Duncan, whose various family members lived in the house over the decades. (The Merrimans and

Duncans had married into the Rice family.) The house went vacant in the 1970s, but got a new life when Waller and her then-husband, Jim, bought it in 1990 to open as a tea room. The inn concept started two years later, to make more use of the spacious home.

There was something odd about the house almost from the beginning. The couple, who were career U.S. Navy, were looking at several locations to relocate to across the country. Jim saw a picture of the house and said it felt like déjà vu. One of Waller's brothers lived in Newberry and checked out the house for them, and her husband again had the strange feeling while looking at the pictures the brother sent. They eventually bought the house after a few visits, and soon saw there may have been something to the déjà vu experience. They found a picture of Thomas Duncan, who lived in the house in the 1880s, and he looked just like Jim.

Not that they believed in reincarnation, but it set the tone for what happened next.

Peggy's brother Mark came to help with the renovation process. They were working in the dining room area, and Mark kept turning his head to look at something. Peggy asked her brother what he was looking at, and he replied he kept seeing a woman wearing a blue-gray dress with a bustle on it walking back and forth in the next room. He couldn't see all of her and never caught more than a glimpse. He didn't realize he was seeing a ghost. Peggy never saw the woman, but a clairvoyant who came to stay at the Merridun a few years after it opened said the ghost was Peggy's guardian spirit. Her name was Mary Ann, and she had lived in the house in the 1880s. She chose to watch over Peggy to make sure she was safe.

Mary Ann, though, wasn't the only one helping out.

Peggy said she and her ex-husband chose some odd colors for the walls during the renovation process, and that friends kept saying they were the wrong ones for such an antebellum home. These were colors and floral patterns that didn't quite make sense and appeared to clash, but for some reason Peggy knew these were the right colors. She soon got an insight into what may have sparked the strange palate. As they peeled back decades of wallpaper and paint, they found the early colors in several rooms. They matched the ones Peggy had chosen.

The clairvoyant said Mr. and Mrs. Duncan also had watched over the renovation process and still monitor work done on the house. They are two of the ten ghosts in the home. The medium also introduced Peggy to several other ghosts roaming the Merridun. There are two Native Americans, who are likely members of the Cherokee tribe that once populated the Upstate, but it is unknown why they stay at the Merridun. They protect the guests and travelers who come to the inn. There are also a young boy and girl who often play in the dining room. They are rarely noticed, but the clairvoyant said the children often play games there. One guest, who didn't know about the two ghosts, told Peggy she always had the sudden urge to hop and skip when in the room. Was she feeling the urge of the ghost children?

Then there is a red-haired woman named Margaret, who also keeps to herself, but her small, white dog is a well-known visitor. Peggy said she has had numerous run-ins with the dog, such as feeling it jump onto beds when no one else was around or eating food laid out for the cat.

"I'll hear something munching on the cat food and think it's my cat, D.J.," she explained. "But then I realize D.J. is curled up in a chair or next to me."

People have also heard something run through the cat door and expected to see D.J., but instead just found the door flapping slightly. One time, Peggy distinctly felt something furry rub around her leg. She looked down expecting to see her cat. Again, nothing was there.

The final ghost is a black woman, who is believed to have been a nursemaid. The clairvoyant said the woman is usually behind the house and watches over children in the home much like she did in her life.

With this much activity and watching over going on, the

ghosts need to unwind every now and then. Peggy said that a few years ago she could hear voices coming from downstairs via an intercom system she had installed during the renovations. Her mother was in one of the first-floor rooms at the time, so Peggy went downstairs to see if she had gotten up and was talking to guests staying during the Christmas season. No one was stirring, not even the cat, who was curled up on a living room couch.

"It sounded like they were having a Christmas party down there," she said.

Were the ghosts taking a break from their year-round haunting, or was it some leftover imprint from the home's many fond Christmases past?

There have been other minor occurrences. Guests have said they locked the doors to their rooms before going to sleep only to wake up and have all three deadbolts unlatched even though they had heard nothing overnight. Other visitors have asked Peggy if staff were moving furniture during the night because they heard someone lugging something heavy up and down the steps. Each time the answer was an obvious no, which has drawn raised eyebrows from more than one guest. And finally, a former employee could constantly be heard exclaiming, "What?" while walking around the building. When Peggy asked her what was going on, the woman replied that she always felt like someone was looking over her shoulder. She thought it was her boss at first, but never saw anything. She was getting annoyed so she kept saying what.

Peggy also added that there is probably a small fortune in pennies beneath the carpets. The ghosts apparently leave the coins in very conspicuous places. Peggy thought someone was playing tricks at first, but soon couldn't explain how the pennies would appear in locked rooms where she had been the only person to enter or exit. The clairvoyant advised Peggy to put the pennies under the carpets for good luck.

"Who knows how many pennies I've stuck under rugs," she said.

There have been enough sightings and occurrences over the years that Peggy now keeps a ghost journal at the front desk. She never tells guests about the ghosts when they check in, but before they leave she asks if anything unusual happened during their stay. Quite a few people have written along the book's lines.

"It's been a while since I had it out," she said. "Maybe I need to get it back out soon."

The Devil's Castle
Numerous Stories Surround Former Hospital

Who would think a park full of playground equipment and soccer fields would have a ghost story attached to it? Let alone a story that incurs the name The Devil's Castle. Well, for residents of one Greenville community, that ghost story rings true even though the surroundings may seem more children's book than ghost book.

Before a fire destroyed the old Greenville Tuberculosis Hospital in 2002, the building at 220 Beverly Road on Piney Mountain had garnered the sinister name of The Devil's Castle because of all the odd goings-on people reported seeing there over the years. Strange lights at night, séances, oddly formed dark shapes moving across the lawn—all were frequent sights at the slightly gothic-style building. It closed as a hospital in the 1950s, but served as a work release center for prisoners from 1974 until 1997.

Residents around the old hospital are somewhat unwilling to talk about what used to go on there except to say something always seemed to be happening that couldn't be explained. But people who visited the site often have chilling stories to tell. Doug Ray remembered he and his friends once took a Ouija board to the old building one night in the late 1990s, just after the facility closed for good.

"We were just going up there for a laugh. We had heard stories about flashing lights and ghostly moans, but we thought it was just superstition," he said.

44

They parked their car down near Rutherford Road so passing cops wouldn't get suspicious, seeing a car outside the abandoned building. They didn't need a flashlight because it was midsummer and the moon was high in the sky. Walking up the small hill, they crossed the street and stepped onto the old grass courtyard around the property. Maybe it was just nerves or a faulty memory, but Ray swears he started to get colder as he approached the building. He had to rub his bare forearms a couple of times to get the hairs to stay down.

They nosed around the front entrance of the building looking for an opening. Every step they took seemed to crunch loudly on the grass and rocks. One of the group pulled a small, silver flashlight from his pocket and shined it through one of the old windows. Graffiti and cobwebs filled the rooms. They all agreed the building was probably too dangerous to enter.

"We got kind of spooked, so we stopped looking inside and decided to set up behind the building in a thicket of trees," he said.

The foursome found a small clearing and set up the board on the ground. One of the friends had bought the Ouija in a store in Asheville, and it had all kinds of strange runes on it. This wasn't an ordinary Parker Brothers version. One of the guys said he would keep lookout because he had heard a Ouija didn't work well with four people.

"He was lying about hearing that, but we let him hang back," Ray recalled. "He was just too spooked by what was going on."

So, the three of them knelt around the board and put their hands on it. Almost immediately, the planchette started to move. It was forming a question for them. It wanted to know who they were. The guy who had brought the board said he had never seen anything like this before. He asked the spirit to identify who it was instead. The three felt the planchette slide to the "no" answer. Ray's friend said they should break contact. He had used the board before, but he had never experienced such a hostile force.

45

"As soon he said that, the planchette's little glass part shattered," Ray recalled.

They pulled their hands away from the board and stood staring at it with a mix of shock and disbelief. Their silence was broken when the friend who refused to play the Ouija yelled out, "Guys, there's something behind you!"

"We all turned our heads and there was something walking toward us through the trees. It was making a kind of humming noise. That's all we really needed to see and hear to know we needed to get out of there," Ray said.

They ran toward the road, with their lookout dashing at least one hundred feet ahead of them. As they ran, they could hear strange noises in the trees, and Ray said he felt like he was going to be trapped in the woods forever. His heart pumped more out of fear than from the fact he was running as fast his legs could carry him. When they got to the road, they turned around. They could see clearly where their Ouija board had been left behind. It appeared to glow for a second in the moonlight and then fade. The woods became very dark again. Out of breath, they all kind of laughed a little bit, but then they realized that their buddy who had refused to use the board wasn't there anymore. They walked down the hill toward Rutherford Road, but they couldn't see him anywhere. When they got to their car he wasn't there either.

They decided to get in the car and see if they could find him, figuring it would be faster than looking on foot. The last anyone had seen him he was running through the woods with them. They drove around the area for a few minutes, but couldn't see him anywhere. They nervously thought to go back into the woods to look for him. Maybe he had fallen. Just as they decided to drive toward the old building, one of them saw him out of the corner of his eye. He was running toward Wade Hampton Boulevard on Pleasantburg Drive.

"We got him in the car and he said he had gotten so scared in the woods, he just kept running," Ray recalled. "Lucky for him, he wasn't that fast of a runner or we would have never found him."

46

The area where the teens had gone was often littered with Satanic markings, said a Greenville County sheriff's deputy, who asked that his name be kept anonymous. The deputy felt that the paintings and things left behind were made by people trying to scare nearby residents, but inside the old building was a different story. Deputies used to meet there on early weekend mornings if there were no other calls, to practice entering a building and to learn ways of handling situations. The building was ideal because it was abandoned, but in good enough condition that the deputies didn't have to worry about any accidents. They could also get rid of any unwanted trespassers since the building was a popular place for teens to look for ghosts.

But it was ghosts the deputies heard more often than any living creatures.

The deputies generally did a sweep of the building when they first entered, looking for anyone who might be stowed away inside, before doing drills. The building was usually pitch black, with only the deputies' heavy Maglites providing a way to see. Many of the doors were padlocked or blocked off. Yet, as soon as the deputies would gather again on the first floor they would hear what sounded like footsteps coming from the second floor. As they climbed the ramp and swept their lights through the corridors, they could hear indistinct voices. Somewhat like whispers. Never enough for the deputies to understand, but enough for them to just hear it. However, the deputies knew there was no living thing in the building.

"We were always told the place was haunted," the deputy said. "I believe it."

Most of the problems with the site ended in mid-2002 when a horrific fire brought a final end to the decaying building. The cause of the fire was never determined. The property didn't remain vacant for long. Greenville County Council decided to turn the site into a park the following year even though some of the ruins of the old building were still visible. Some of the old stonework fences were built into the park's landscape and now give the park an old-time feel.

47

Although there are no further reports of strange things being seen there at night, the next time you feel like a good game of soccer, maybe you should just think twice about where you are playing. It could be built over the ruins of The Devil's Castle.

Anna of Anderson College
Does the Ghost of a Former College President's Daughter Still Haunt the School?

Another ghost whose story is based in fact is that of Anna, the teenage daughter of a former Anderson College president in the 1920s. Anna was dating someone her father did not approve of, according to the legend most often told by students and faculty. The reason for the disagreement stems from the fact that she was a Baptist and the young man was a Roman Catholic. Religious friction was somewhat common in the South in the 1920s, and Anderson College was strongly associated with the Baptist faith at the time.

The family's residence was one of the oldest buildings on campus, and it featured a grand staircase in the front foyer. The father and daughter had a fight, and the college president removed his daughter's engagement ring and tossed it out one of the building's windows. To get a measure of revenge for this cruel act, the daughter planned to fake her own hanging off the second-floor landing. She hoped to scare her father into giving his approval. Unfortunately, the trick did not work as planned and she hanged herself.

Since then, dozens of students and faculty members have reported seeing the spirit of Anna, not only in the building, but also roaming the front lawn of the college. Students have even said the ghost of Anna played tricks on them. One student who attended the school in the 1980s said the stories of Anna were rampant and usually made the rounds among freshmen during the Halloween season. The former student I talked to didn't want her name used, but she said several of her friends reported seeing stuff late at night. One year several of them tried to sneak into the building at Halloween, but they were thwarted by security.

"I hate to think what we would have seen if we actually got inside the building," she said. "I'm really thankful for that security guard because I really didn't want to go in, but I didn't want to seem a chicken to my friends."

The two-story structure is one of seven brick buildings that make up the front entrance to the college, located close to downtown Anderson. Situated at the far right, it was donated to the college in 1914 to serve as the president's residence. The building eventually became known as the Sullivan Music Building and housed the school's music program until 1994. It now serves as part of the campus ministry program, and a chapel is featured inside. Anna can often be seen on the staircase, as well as in the choir room, which was added to the building sometime before 1990.

School officials, for the record, don't talk about the ghost, but they admitted there is evidence that a former college president's daughter did die while living on campus in the 1920s. They would not say if the death was a suicide or not.

"It's not something that we tell incoming students, but we know students talk about it," said Barry Ray, a school spokesman.

Anderson College made the transition to Anderson University in 2005. It remains to be seen whether Anna has made the transition as well. Ray said the Sullivan Building can be a bit spooky at night and joked that he never wanted his office moved to the building.

"I don't like walking by it late at night," he said.

Strange Tales from Stumphouse Tunnel
What Lurks Inside the Mountain?

The first thing that most visitors notice when getting close to Stumphouse Tunnel is the rapid drop in temperature, regardless of whether they believe in ghosts or not. The temperature just seems to drop ten degrees when they get within about twenty-five feet of the cavern that cuts into Stumphouse Mountain, about five miles north of Walhalla in Oconee County.

And then a low moan comes from the tunnel. A rational person knows it's just the wind echoing off the cavern walls, but the haunting tune seems to be that of a voice calling from beyond the grave. Is it a warning from the men who worked in the tunnel decades before, or something more sinister? And what about tales of a little man who sits in the tunnel entrance at night and plays catch with passersby? Or recordings of voices talking in the tunnel when no one else is there?

There are a lot of legends about Stumphouse Tunnel—but to start, let's tell the story of how this tunnel into the mountain came to be. In 1850, the Blue Ridge Rail Line undertook the ambitious project of building a railroad from Charleston to Cincinnati, Ohio. The line made it as far as the present-day city of Walhalla, which in fact was settled by the German Colonization Society in anticipation of the area's becoming a major destination for travelers. However, giant Stumphouse Mountain loomed in the distance. Planners decided to cut through the mountain and then continue the line on the other side. It would then connect to a series of planned tunnels leading under the

Blue Ridge Mountains. More than fifteen hundred Irish immigrant workers converged on the site with sledgehammers, pick-axes, and black powder to cut a roughly thirty-foot-high, thirty-foot-wide tunnel some 5,863 feet into the mountain. Four shafts were blasted through the top of the mountain to give the workers air. Many of the men lived in a small town created to support the workers. It was simply called Tunnel Hill.

The work was slow going to say the least. At peak capacity, workers were only able to get two hundred feet a month. Money was also tight. The original group financing the plan backed out in 1852, and the State of South Carolina took over in hopes of getting the line to the Tennessee Valley. By 1859, the workers had only gotten about sixteen hundred feet when the state stopped granting money. The Civil War erupted, and the plan was abandoned for the duration of the conflict.

The plan was scuttled altogether after the war, and the idea and the tunnel were eventually forgotten by most people in the state. Tunnel Hill, which at one time had more saloons than churches, became a ghost town after the workers left for other pursuits. People still find old artifacts, such as shovels and pieces of slate, left over from the townspeople.

The Pendleton District Commission eventually closed Stumphouse Tunnel due to rock slides, and then turned it and the surrounding forest area over to the city of Walhalla. Walhalla, which now operates the site, reopened the tunnel in the spring of 2000 as part of a state park.

The tunnel also has something of an edible history. Because the temperature is around 50 degrees and the humidity is about 85 percent year-round, a professor at Clemson University decided to temporarily store and age blue cheese there. The environment of the tunnel was later duplicated in the Clemson Agricultural Center, and the cheese making was moved there.

And of course there were ghost tales associated with Stumphouse Tunnel. One of the stranger legends states that if you go to the tunnel late at night during certain times of the year, you can get involved in an odd game of catch. The story goes that if you throw a ball into the cave entrance, the ball will bounce back out to you. Some people have stated they have actually seen a little man come forward and toss the ball back. No one knows who or what he is, or why this would happen.

A group of paranormal researchers visited Stumphouse in 2001. They claimed to make a recording inside the tunnel of a female spirit that said, "those guides. There's no problem left until the spirituals leave the grave." The group later captured the strange echoes of a man's voice that states, "We're here." It is not known who the man and woman might be.

Regardless of ghost legends, Stumphouse Tunnel is a pretty creepy place even during daylight hours. It is located in the far northern corner of South Carolina, in Oconee County. The entrance to the park is a winding road, like a snake slithering down a mountainside, just off Highway 28. An old, faded sign stating "Stumphouse Tunnel" hangs over the gravel parking lot just before the small hill that leads to the cavern entrance.

Giant tree roots cling to boulders along the sides of the cavern, and depending on the weather there is any number of little waterfalls flowing down the sides. The temperature drops once you get into the shadow of the tunnel entrance, and then there is the eerie wail from inside. The first part of the cave is still light enough to see without using a flashlight. Water trickles down the rock walls, across what almost appear to be faces etched into the mountainside. If you look hard enough you will see little bits of brown, bristly fur jutting out of some of the crevices. Those are baby bats taking a nap in the tunnel walls. The water pouring in creates an almost sandbar effect down the middle of the tunnel. After only a few dozen steps, the darkness starts to surround you. You can see what's immediately in front of you, but your feet and hands are practically invisible.

The daylight at the entrance grows farther and farther away as you walk, until it seems just a speck in the distance. After walking about three hundred feet, you come to an ancient brick wall with a little doorway cut into the side. A cold, iron gate is always open at the door. The brick wall is covered in graffiti by local teens. One spray-painted sign on the wall simply states "Beware."

The sun completely vanishes after crossing through the iron gate and into the second chamber. The only visible light comes from a hole in the ceiling from which a steady drizzle of rain falls. The closer you get to the light, the brighter the surroundings get. It is one of the air holes cut into the rock more than 150 years ago. Walking forward, the cavern quickly becomes dark again until you suddenly come upon a second brick wall. This wall is also graffiti-covered, but its door does not have a gate. Crossing into this chamber puts you into complete darkness. The light from the ventilation shaft is extinguished behind the wall.

A flashlight is needed from this point forward, but you may want to be careful. You never know who or what you might find in Stumphouse Tunnel. And be sure to take a ball.

Hangman's Noose Road
Does the Ghost of Willie Earle Still Haunt Greenville?

Susan Ellis isn't someone who scares easily or believes in a lot of ghost stories. But a couple of incidents that happened when she was a young woman left an indelible mark on her memory and make her believe ghost tales just a little. They involve one of Greenville's most famous ghosts.

Ellis was in high school in the late 1970s and dating the man she would later marry. They decided one night to drive down Old Bramlett Road, just off of White Horse Road. Friends of theirs had told them a story about the ghost of a black man who was shot and beaten to death by a lynch mob years before. The friends told them they had seen the image of a man hanging limply from a tree in the woods one night. Among teens, the road was morbidly referred to as "Hangman's Noose Road."

Susan and Tim parked their car at the edge of the nearly pitch-black woods. The air was still and quiet, then they heard something in the woods. It sounded like a faint rustle of leaves and they tensed up a little bit. They wondered what was out there. An animal? Their friends? Or maybe the ghost?

The noise grew stronger. It seemed as if it was getting closer, but they couldn't see anything beyond a few feet. Tim flipped on the car's headlights.

There was nothing there.

That was all the couple needed to not see. They backed the car away from the woods and sped down the road until they saw streetlights again. Even though they were scared, they returned two more times in the next few weeks to see if maybe their imagination had gotten the best of them. Or maybe if it was their friends who had played a prank. Each time they had the same experience. Something large was walking through the woods toward them, but it was invisible to their eyes.

It is possible Ellis and her friends had had a modern-day encounter with the spectral ghost of Willie Earle, a black man who was lynched in 1947 by a mob of taxicab drivers in the woods near there. When people mention Greenville ghost legends, the stories almost always start with Willie Earle.

The sad tale behind the ghost started when Earle was accused of killing a cab driver while getting a ride in February 1947. Earle was a strapping twenty-four-year-old. He held several odd jobs, including working as a plumber. His footprints were tracked to a small house in Liberty, but he also had two addresses in Greenville. He was arrested and brought to the Pickens County Jail, which incidentally has a ghost story of its own told earlier in this book. A group of taxi drivers angry over the death of their friend wanted justice for themselves, however. This was still a decade before the civil rights movement became a major cause in the South, and animosity between the races was high. Lynch mobs were still a very real threat to blacks.

The angry mob, many of whom carried shotguns, drove out of Greenville late one night and made their way to Pickens. They descended on the tiny jail and ordered the beleaguered sheriff to hand over Earle. Jailer Ed Gilstrap stood firm but soon realized he was outmatched. Did he want this angry crowd attacking his county residents instead? He handed Earle over to the mob, who threw him, bound and gagged, into a taxicab trunk and headed down the Easley Highway.

But instead of taking Earle to the Greenville County Jail, they took a left onto White Horse Road. They soon took another left onto Old Bramlett Road. Then the mob pulled him from the cab and started to beat him. One man took a knife to

Earle—cutting him along the same lines of his alleged victim. Another man shot at Earle, hitting him once, possibly twice. The entire time, he struggled to get away and screamed that he was innocent. His pleas fell on deaf ears, and Willie Earle died in the small patch of woods that early February morning. The crowd dispersed, leaving his body lying there. Someone would later call a funeral home to say a black man's body was in the woods.

In the 1940s, that normally would have been the end of the story, but something strange happened. Prosecutors tried to bring the lynch mob to justice. That was unheard of at the time and created a major sensation. However, all thirty-one men accused of being involved in the killing were acquitted. But apparently Willie Earle was less forgiving.

For years to come, cab drivers across Greenville would tell hushed tales of getting calls out to Old Bramlett Road. Most drivers knew there were not many homes out there at the time. In fact, the area was known for its remoteness. An old slaughter yard and a rock quarry were there, but not much else. Nonetheless, they would take the fare from dispatch without a thought. Finding nothing when they got there, they would inevitably get out of the car to see if their would-be passenger was injured and nearby. That's when they would hear the voices. Angry voices. The voices of a mob playing out over the chill night air. And then they would hear the voice of a man calling out for help and begging for mercy. And finally, according to the legends passed on by drivers, a black form would slowly start coming out of the woods.

At that point, the drivers would scramble back to their cars and go speeding down the road. Just like Susan Ellis did when she and her boyfriend had their nights interrupted all those years ago.

However, Ellis notes that her friends had only part of the story right. There was definitely something going in those woods, but Earle had never been hanged.

"I think our friends got part of the story wrong along the way," she said years later.

And while Ellis and her husband gave up checking out old haunted roads, taking up fishing instead, it was not their only experience with ghosts, she recalled. Fishing proved as scary as courting on at least one trip.

Years after the stirrings at Hangman's Noose Road, they were driving through Waterloo on the way to Lake Greenwood when they saw a man standing on the side of the road near a cemetery. They slowed down to ask the man for directions. The man stared at them blankly for a second. His brown pants and tan shirt were tattered and torn, and his eyes had almost a milky white look.

Susan's husband, Tim, described the chilling encounter and how he asked the man several questions but could not get a response. He remembered the encounter lasting almost a minute before he decided to drive off when it appeared the glassy-eyed man was going to come toward the car. And then, in an instant, the man vanished into thin air.

"That was the closest I've ever come to seeing a zombie," he said. Susan also described the being as looking almost like a zombie.

"That was probably the scariest moment of my life," she said.

Martha Walker
Does the Head Mistress of a Spartanburg School Still Roam the Grounds?

It was like a trip down memory lane for Lawrence Sloan that quickly turned a sharp right onto terror drive. Sloan was working on the South Carolina School for the Deaf and Blind's museum project late one night in the mid-1980s. He had been a student at the school and later served as its historian for almost fifty years, so going through boxes of old pictures and artifacts brought back a lot of fond memories.

Newton Pinckney Walker and his wife, Martha, founded the school in 1849 near the site of two Revolutionary War battles. The school's oldest building, Walker Hall, is named after the family.

Walker Hall is the school's administration office now, and the hub of all that goes on at the large, picturesque campus just south of Spartanburg's city limits. At three stories high and with large columns out front, the building is a perfect example of antebellum construction. A large, central stairwell connects the three floors. It is intricately carved and forms a square that is the building's focal point.

But it is the ghost story that makes Walker Hall a little bit more interesting.

It was a little after midnight when Sloan, who was on the second floor of Walker Hall, saw something breeze past an open door just out of the corner of his eye. He didn't think anything of it. Probably just a figment of his imagination. So he returned to poring over the collection spread out before him on a large desk in a side conference room.

And then he saw it again, but this time it had passed in the opposite direction. He figured his friends were playing a trick on him. With numerous windows lining the front of the building, he also figured it could have been the lights of a car going by. But he wanted to make sure.

Sloan pushed back his chair and raised himself up. He was going to see whoever it was scurrying around the building at such a late hour. He walked out into the hallway and turned a corner. What he saw would haunt him for years to come. The vision of Martha Walker stood before him plain as anything he had ever seen. Her hair was pulled back in a tight bun and parted down the middle. She had a large brooch at her neck, and she wore an impeccably crisp white blouse.

Sloan is deaf, and using sign language he found the best word he could think of to describe her: Ghostly.

"I was just terrified," he said, using his hands.

The apparition looked at him and waved warmly. Sloan easily recognized Walker from working on the museum project. Her picture had been everywhere in the archives. Was she just checking in to say she approved of his work? Sloan wasn't about to find out. He had seen enough at this point and went back to the room with all of the photographs. He grabbed his belongings, turned off the lights, and headed to his room in another building.

Martha Walker had been a dynamo in the early years of the school, records show. Three of her siblings were among the initial students, and Walker herself taught. Her husband died in 1861, and she guided the school through the turmoil of the Civil War, when many other small schools closed. When much of South Carolina was ravaged by wartime famine, she fed students using her own food.

She also raised seven children and for a spell lived inside Walker Hall, which was completed in 1859 and was known as

Main Hall until the 1950s. The family's apartment was on the second floor, where Sloan saw her years later.

It would be almost a decade before he told anyone what he had seen. He figured it was just too amazing a story to pass on, even if he was one of the most respected people at the school.

"People would have thought I had gone crazy if I told them that story," he said.

However, Sloan wasn't the only one who had heard or seen Walker's presence, as he soon learned. Some students claimed to have even snapped pictures of Walker—or at least some being—looking out of the windows over the years. The students claimed the photos were not rigged and that no one—at least no one living—was supposed to be in the building when the photos were taken from outside.

A reporter from a local newspaper even spent a night in Walker Hall, but alas her subsequent article said nothing happened. Rumors floated around the school for the next few years of people hearing strange noises or of things going missing. Some speculated that it was the ghost of Martha Walker.

"That started to make me feel better about it," he said.

As the school's historian, Sloan has come to love telling stories about the school's old days. Walking along the hardwood floors of Walker Hall, he points to where a pipe organ once sat or where students used to cook or learn to sew. It is clear that he loves the building and the school very deeply.

And while telling the story relieved some of his concerns, it did not alleviate any of his fears of going into the old building at night. He won't stay after dark anymore. It was just once, but he was spooked. One time he was crossing campus after dinner and went the long way so as to avoid the building. He just didn't want to be near it.

As soon as darkness falls, he makes his way down the grand wooden staircases and goes home. He loves the building. He just doesn't love ghosts.

The Witch's Tree
A Chilling Tale from Northern Greenville

Highway 11 runs about 120 miles from the Georgia-South Carolina border to the Cherokee County line. The road was once a Cherokee Indian trading route, but the legend of the Witch's Tree doesn't go back to that time.

The tree is located just past where the highway crosses from Pickens County to Greenville County. The gnarled, old tree has to be at least forty feet high, with limbs shooting off in all directions. It is about a half-mile from the road and stands in the middle of a large clearing in the woods. And according to some people familiar with the area, it is the site of a great deal of hauntings.

"It's kind of one of those hidden legends," said Ed Jasper, a local ghost chaser.

Jasper has heard a lot of tales about the site: that it may be connected to Indian legends and spirits; that it is the burial spot for a powerful witch; that it is the burial spot for a long-lost traveler.

"There are quite a few stories out there," he said. "I don't know which one may be true, but I have seen some strange things out there."

Jasper remembers first hearing about the tree from a friend in the early 1990s and getting intrigued. The story he was told at the time was that a witch from Charleston chose the spot as the place for her burial during the Civil War. She was convinced her home was going to be overrun by Yankee soldiers, so she decided to head to the mountains to practice her spells and hexes away from enemy eyes. However, the legend stated the woman died en route or perhaps was killed by some of her followers, who came to disbelieve some of her claims.

Either way, they buried her in the rural spot and planted a seedling over her grave to mark the location. The tree grew, but it is not known if her followers ever came back to honor their former guru. The friend told Jasper that the tree grew quickly, but that it never blooms properly.

In the spring the tree gets numerous blooms and buds, but most die out before maturing. The blooms that survive become unusually brittle and all fall off by late August regardless of what grows nearby. That said, not that much grows around the tree. The clearing is about thirty-five feet in diameter, a nearly perfect circle. The grass is green in the summer, but there is never any trace of the leaves falling from the old tree. In addition, birds and squirrels are never seen on the tree despite being in abundance in the surrounding forest. In the fall, the tree looks blackened, as if it has withstood a scorching inferno that could not topple it.

Faced with a story like that, Jasper couldn't wait to get on the road and go looking for the tree one fall morning just two days before Halloween. He figured if he wanted to see something out in the woods, Halloween would be the perfect time of year to try. It was just after 11 A.M. and the sun was high in the sky and shining brightly when he found the pull off near the side of the road where his friend had told him to go. Jasper was an avid hiker at the time, so he carried a lot of gear in the back of his old Jeep Waggoneer to aid in an emergency.

"I was a little nervous because I didn't know what I was looking for out there," he said. "On a hike, you know how far you are going and you can prepare that way. On this, I didn't even know what the name of the witch was."

He pulled out his battered knapsack and packed some granola bars and a jug of water. He also threw in some strong rope, a compass, a rain poncho, an emergency kit, and a small survival knife. Jasper left his vehicle on the side of the road and soon started hiking in the general direction his friend has told him. After about an hour of hiking up and down, he came upon a clearing. He was facing back toward the road and could see a large tree in the middle of the area. As he approached it, he soon realized this had to be the tree.

It was as bare as anything else in the woods, but it had a look of being charred black. He felt compelled to close in on the tree. He became audibly aware that his feet were not crunching any leaves on the ground. It was as if the area had been cleared of them. He got to the base of the tree and looked up through its thick, clingy limbs. The sun overhead seemed to dip in and out of the tree through the branches waving in the wind. He wanted to see what the blackened bark felt like. He reached out a tentative hand toward the tree.

He heard a snap.

Jasper whirled around to see if someone else might have been in the woods and instinctively crouched down to where his knees almost scraped the woodland floor. He couldn't see anyone nearby. It must have been a squirrel, he thought, or some other forest creature.

But then he realized that there were no animals around. No telltale sounds of a squirrel jumping from branch to branch. He needed to get a hold of himself for a second, he remembered. This was just a tree! He took off his pack and laid it on the ground.

He was probably letting his imagination run away with him. He stood himself up and again reached for the tree. He could feel his arm shaking as his fingertips neared the bark. He half expected to hear a branch snap again, but instead he felt a regular old tree.

He blew a sigh of relief.

However, Jasper soon began to notice it had gotten very dark out. The sun, which a few seconds before appeared to be overhead, was now heading toward the tree line around the clearing. How long had he been there at the tree?

He grabbed his backpack, hurled it over his shoulders, and started jogging back toward the road. If he followed a straight line he knew he would be okay. The farther he got away from the tree, the darker the forest seemed to be getting. He started to feel like he was being watched. He could soon see the road, but he could not see his vehicle. He broke into a full run to make it to the road.

Jasper broke through a small clump of brambles and fell knees and palms first onto the pavement. Not even thinking, he looked up and down for his Jeep. He noticed a sign on the side of the road and soon realized he was about a mile away from his vehicle. Again, he felt relieved, even though it was getting darker by the second. He decided he needed to do something about the abrasions on his palms and knees before walking any further.

He slung his pack from his shoulders and reached inside. He found nothing.

The emergency kit, compass, rope, water, granola bars, poncho, and knife were all missing. He knew he had packed them in the truck when he set out. He had taken out his compass at one point to get his bearings.

"There was just nothing there," he said. "That really freaked me out. There is a lot of things about that hike I can't explain, but that is the weirdest."

Jasper added he never returned to look for the tree.

"That is just one thing I never want to go through again," he said.

A Ghost Story 122 Years in the Making
A Young Woman's Arrival
Sparks a Ghost's Appearance

The family was staying in Abbeville only for a short time while the father worked there in 1984. To pass the time one day, the mother and one of her daughters decided to walk the streets of Abbeville's charming downtown. Turning onto Trinity Street, the girl, who was about eighteen at time, broke into a full sprint toward the large, stone-walled church at the bottom of the hill.

As the mother tried to catch up, she could see the teen was talking to someone and appeared agitated. The mother could not see anyone, though. When the girl, whose name was Dana, started to cry, her mother became even more concerned. What was happening to her daughter? And then Dana turned to her mother and said, "Her name is Elizabeth, and she's in a terrible situation. We need to help her."

So started one of the strangest ghost stories ever told in Abbeville, said May Hutchinson, Trinity Church's historian. That is a lot to say, considering Abbeville is a small town with a lot of ghosts floating around.

Dana soon explained what had happened. She said that as she turned the corner she saw a woman with long, dark hair standing in the courtyard of the church crying hysterically. The woman was wearing nineteenth century-style clothing. When Dana saw her, she felt compelled to run to her and see what the problem was. Dana could never explain why she felt such immediate empathy for someone she didn't know. The woman was apparently surprised to see Dana as well. She told Dana that her name was Elizabeth and that she had been killed more than 120 years earlier, inside Trinity Church. No one had noticed her sobbing before.

Over the next few days, Dana returned to the church several times and spoke to Elizabeth and got more information about what had happened. According to Dana, Elizabeth had lived in Abbeville at the outbreak of the Civil War with her husband, Drew, and young son, Jacob. Drew went off to war in 1861 like many young Southern men, and Elizabeth took Jacob every day to Trinity to pray for her husband's return. One day she heard some men talking loudly in the back of the church. They were talking about gold and using words she felt were inappropriate for a House of God. The men saw Elizabeth look back at them and figured she had overheard what they were conspiring about. She was really just trying to get them to watch their manners.

The men started to make threatening gestures toward her and Jacob. Being an intelligent woman and able to determine it was a dangerous situation, she picked up her son and ran for the exit. The men, unfortunately, were too fast and blocked her escape. During a tussle, they grabbed Jacob, who screamed for his mother's arms, and rushed him out of the church.

Before leaving, the men warned Elizabeth that if she told anyone about what they were planning, she would never see Jacob again. Elizabeth begged them to let the boy go and swore she hadn't heard what they were talking about. Before the men could ever accomplish what they were plotting, young Jacob died. Elizabeth didn't know if they had killed him or if the boy had died of natural causes. Furious, she ran to the church and confronted the conspirators. She begged them to at least tell her where they had buried him, but they refused. When she grabbed one of the men by the shirt to push him, she saw another one raise some kind of weapon.

The next thing she remembered she was laying on the floor of the church with the men standing around her. She got up, but looked down to the floor to see her body still there, motionless. Elizabeth was dead, but her ghost remained. Stuck in this world without a body, she roamed to see if she could find her husband on the battlefield. But again, she was too late. Drew had died in the Second Battle of Manassas in 1862. Elizabeth returned to Abbeville to stay at Trinity, where she had found so much solace in her short life, hoping someone would one day see her. But 122 years had passed before that August day when young Dana ventured down Trinity Street.

As one might guess, there was a lot of speculation as to the truth of the story. A search of county records couldn't find anyone who matched the identities of Elizabeth, Drew, or Jacob, Hutchinson recalled years later. But many believed the girl had seen something at the church. The reason? Elizabeth had told Dana the names and descriptions of her killers. After a lengthy search, a set of dusty old records was found that matched the names and descriptions Dana gave. It was a search that no eighteen-year-old girl there for only a few weeks ever could have accomplished, so many reasoned someone or something had tipped Dana off to the story. It was a mystery, but it spawned ghost talk.

As for Dana and Elizabeth, there was a happy ending. Dana found young Jacob's grave for Elizabeth, which finally brought Elizabeth peace. And while Dana and Elizabeth never understood how or why they met each other, Dana said Elizabeth was going to stay at Trinity for a while, waiting to see if anyone else was going to see her.

Hutchinson said she has often told the story of Elizabeth and Dana for young people, acting out the key parts, such as the abduction of Jacob and Elizabeth's death. And while the story captivates those in attendance, no one has reported seeing Elizabeth again. Did she finally leave, or is she just waiting for someone like Dana to come again and talk for a while? And if that person does come along, it would be interesting to see what she has to say.

The Ghost of the Colony Theater
Film Projector or Something Else?

Jerry Manchester had to look twice because he didn't believe what he had seen. There in the window at the Colony Theater was a woman with a faint glow around her.

It was just a few weeks before Halloween 1989, and a slight nip was in the air in downtown Easley. Manchester was driving back from a Clemson football game to his home in Greenville. While not the route most football fans take, he preferred to go this way because he liked to drive through the quaint downtown. He especially liked the old movie theater's 1950s-style glass-bulbs marquee, so he would often take a look at it as he passed by, even if was dark, which it was that night. He saw the woman when he was almost parallel with the building.

"I never saw anyone in those windows ever, so it kind of surprised me," he recalled years later. "I turned my head to look because I knew I saw something."

He remembers that the woman was looking straight out the second-floor window and not really moving. She had a faint glow that made her appear to be dressed all in white. Manchester drove a block down the road and started to question what he had seen. The hairs on the back of his neck and on his arms were erupting in goose pimples despite his wearing a warm sweatshirt.

He had to turn around to see again. Maybe it was a mannequin in the window with a backlight on it. Or a cardboard cutout that was part of a movie promotion. He swung his car around and headed back toward the theater. As he approached the building, he slowed the car to see if anyone was inside.

The window was dark.

As he drove past the two-story brick building heading back toward Clemson, his mind said to turn around again. Maybe somehow the lights from his car had hit something in the window, illuminating it. He turned around again and drove by slowly this time, his head careening toward the window.

Nothing.

Now Manchester started to analyze what was happening in his head. He had been driving about forty miles per hour the first time he went by the building. Maybe he needed to drive that fast again. He turned off the radio in his car and turned around once more. He peeked at the window again, but was concentrating on making another U-turn down the road.

In a few seconds, his car was again facing Greenville and he again drove past the theater. He didn't see anything. For some reason, he swung his car into the little gravel parking lot next to the one-screen theater. He had to know what he'd seen.

"If a cop had come by and seen me doing all this driving back and forth, he would have thought I was nuts," he said.

He took a flashlight from his glove compartment and got out of the car. It was still chilly, but nothing unbearable. He walked to the front of the building and flashed his light up at the window. There was nothing there. He stood there mouth agape for a few moments when he started to see his breath in the night air. No sooner had he seen the effects of the cold, than he felt a chill run down his back.

He turned off his flashlight and ran to his car in a straight sprint. He cranked it up and sped out of the parking lot, shooting up a pile of gravel. He joked later that he would have run all the way back to Greenville if the car hadn't started.

"I was spooked beyond belief," he said.

A few blocks down the road his cold chill was over. He stuck his head out the window to see if it was cold or his imagination. The night air was chilly, but nowhere near as cold as it had been in front of the theater. Manchester was convinced he had seen a ghost.

According to legend, the theater was built on a site where a woman had hanged herself. Many people have heard strange noises in the balcony of the Colony Theater, and a number of locals have seen a woman in the window over the years.

However, John Armistead, whose family ran the theater for twenty-five years, dismissed the story. He never saw or heard anything. He said the story started because the film projector blew a lot of air, and that the air made the white curtains in the room move.

That, he said, is the famed ghost of the Colony Theater. He also said he had never seen any proof that a woman killed herself on the spot before the theater opened in 1948. However, Armistead gave plenty of reasons to look at the old movie house. It is the last of three his family owned in Easley and was designed by famed movie house architect Robert Boller of Kansas City. Armistead's father had met Boller while in Kansas City during World War II.

"There's just no truth to the ghost story," he said.

The Colony Theater closed down in 2002 after having served as a dollar theater for its last few years. The property is now owned by a longtime neighbor, Robinson Funeral Home. Alfred Robinson said he bought the property because its parking lot could serve his funeral home, and so he could preserve the theater as part of Easley history. Its 1948 opening was a major event. He doesn't believe the ghost tales, but he does believe there is another explanation.

"A lot of time memories and ghost stories overlap," he said. "Sometimes people think they see something that is really just in their mind, and after a while it becomes something they can't explain."

David Herman is the pastor of a church that moved into the site after the theater closed. He, too, reports no ghost stories.

"I have been in the building at all hours of the night and haven't seen or heard anything," he said. "It is a dark place at night, so I can see where people get their ideas. But it is just a beautiful building."

Don't try to tell that to Manchester. It was years before he drove through Easley again after that night in 1989. And when he does drive down Highway 8, he keeps his eyes on the road. "I don't want to see anything in that building ever again," he said.

The Strange Presence
Civil War Ghosts in a Wofford College Building

Wofford College is one of those hidden gems of South Carolina. A Methodist college, it dates back to 1854 and has played a major part in the shaping of Spartanburg. Tucked away just a few blocks from downtown's Morgan Square, Wofford has produced generations of Spartanburg and state leaders. For a good portion of the early 2000s, the majority of the State Supreme Court consisted of Wofford graduates.

However, for all of its history and legacy in Spartanburg, Wofford only carries one ghost story. But it's a story that dates back to the school's early years, and it involves the tragic events of the Civil War.

When Benjamin Wofford left money in his will to found the college that bears his name, he envisioned a place that would be a beacon of learning. The campus had six buildings in 1854, and in a testament to the school's roots, five of those buildings are still standing. One of those is the Carlisle-Wallace House, a two-story white brick building in the middle of the campus, and that is where the ghost story starts and finishes. Spartanburg was a railhead prior to the Civil War, which meant a rail line from Charleston ended in downtown Spartanburg. It really was the end of the line for trains, and Spartanburg had built a reputation as a place to stay and relax prior to the war. That reputation played into the war effort, as soldiers wounded in bloody battles such as Sharpsburg needed places to convalesce and heal their wounds. Spartanburg became a destination for many of the South's wounded.

Doyle Boggs, a Wofford College spokesman, said the school became a likely repository for those wounded because it had buildings and a green campus.

"At least some of the college was used for that purpose," he said.

How much of the college and what buildings exactly are unknown, but is very likely the Carlisle-Wallace House was used to house men suffering the effects of gangrene or missing limbs from the deadly conflict. Wofford students played their part in the war. Perhaps some of them even recuperated there after being wounded. The school's ROTC program, the Southern Guards Battalion, claims as its parent unit a group of students who organized themselves into a company of South Carolina volunteers just prior to the Civil War under the leadership of two brothers, Taliferro and Dick Simpson of Pendleton. Their Civil War experiences are described in frequent letters to family and friends.

When South Carolina seceded in December 1860, the young men went to Columbia and volunteered, but were turned down by the governor, who wanted them to finish the 1860–1861 college term. The "Southern Guards" broke up, with some going to their hometowns to enlist, and others becoming part of a Spartanburg unit known as the Palmetto Sharpshooters. Most of them died during the war. Tally Simpson served in the unit until he was killed at the Battle of Chickamauga. Theodosius LeGrand "Addie" Capers, Whiteefoord A. Smith, and J.J. Palmer, messmates in the Palmetto Sharpshooters, were killed by the same artillery shell at the Second Battle of Manassas.

One of the house's main residents during this time was James Carlisle, who started as a history professor but later became the school's third president. In fact, he was one of the school's original professors and lived in the house from 1854 through 1909. He played a major part in shaping Wofford College until he retired as president in 1902.

After his death, a history professor named Wallace moved into the home and lived there for fifty years. It is their two names that give the building its title. The building, though, remained a home for faculty after that. And subsequent residents, including a longtime dean of students, often spoke about somewhat strange things occurring there.

Boggs said they heard noises coming from upstairs in the house, such as skirts rustling, that possibly could be the ghosts of nurses tending to the wounded. The former dean also said he sometimes felt a presence of sorrow.

"Now, he never said he saw something or heard specific things. He never saw specific forms," Boggs said. "It was more of a feeling like something felt on a battlefield."

Roberta Bigger, a modern Wofford dean of students, has heard the spooky stories from former deans over the years. She and her husband, Michael, moved into the house in the mid-1990s, but have reported no strange occurrences. She enjoys staying in the house, but she does take precautions.

"I make sure the doors are locked when I am in the house alone," she said. "I attribute the noises to the fact that it is an old house."

Boggs, who made clear he doesn't believe in ghosts, said it is surprising for a school as old as Wofford to have only one ghost story. He chalked it up to the school's levelheadedness. The school's lush, green campus is one of the first things visitors see when coming into downtown Spartanburg. Its trees and fountains provide a welcome oasis in this rapidly growing Upstate city. It is one of six colleges located in Spartanburg, which has marketed itself as a college town over the years.

Boggs added, though, that campers using the school during summer months started a ghost story one year. The story grew from year to year and quickly gained legend status among each new group coming in.

Boggs couldn't remember specifics about the tale, just that it was made up completely out of the blue. Nor could he remember which group of campers came up with the tale. Perhaps it was the NFL's Carolina Panthers, who have used the school as a summer training facility since their 1995 inception. The team's owner, Jerry Richardson, is a Wofford grad and has been happy to get his alma mater the national exposure each summer.

It's kind of fun to think what NFL greats such as Kevin Greene, Wesley Walls, and Kerry Collins could have come up with during those long days walking around the campus between hot summer practices.

Strange Things Along Highway 107
Oddities Haunt Oconee County Road

I could see the man standing along the side of the road as I slowly drove down the winding two-lane highway just a few miles above Walhalla. His hand reached in the air as if to wave me down for a ride.

Could it be? Could I be looking at the ghost of the Route 107 hitchhiker who has been said to haunt the back roads of Oconee County for more than fifty years? My heart almost leapt into my throat before my senses got the better of me. It was just an old man getting his mail. He must have figured I lived in one of the houses tucked into the mountains that pepper northern Oconee County.

Route 107 snakes through the region, a lush canopy of green forest surrounding the road, and at dusk it can be foreboding as the shadows of trees dance along the pavement. At times a small, silver guardrail is all that protects you from tumbling into one of the steep valleys below. The road has had its share of fatal accidents—and one time when a killer dumped a body on the side of the road—but those aren't part of this ghost story. No, this tale involves, of all things, a plane crash.

The most popular legend about the roadway is the ghost of a man in a flight suit who will attempt to hitch a ride at dusk somewhere between Moody Springs and Lookout Point. He vanishes by the time the driver gets him to his destination. One legend states he is the ghost of a man named David Stephens, whose single-engine plane crashed in the mountains sometime during the 1950s. There is, however, some debate over whether this crash even happened. Some in the area claim it occurred, but there are no surviving records proving it, which leads to speculation about the story.

However, the county museum does record a crash of a B-25 bomber that was on a training run from Mississippi to Greenville during World War II. The plane went down mysteriously in March 1943 and wasn't found for more than a week. And even that was almost by happenstance, as a young boy riding a horse home one day saw the wreckage. Five men died in the crash when the plane apparently hit a mountaintop.

The Oconee Heritage Center has a small display on the wreck, as well as some of the pieces of the bomber that were recovered in late 2005. The plane's gigantic engines are said to still be resting at the bottom of one of the cliffs. Could the man in the airman's suit be one of the five dead B-25 flyers?

Residents also tell tales of the Brown Mountain Lights. These were small, glowing orbs that could be seen in the mountains at night while standing along Route 107 in the 1940s. Residents could never explain them because electricity wasn't available at the time, and this was more than just lanterns or bonfires on mountains several miles away. They are not connected to the Brown Mountain Lights reported in Morganton, North Carolina, but the stories are very similar because they are rarely reported the same way twice, and no one has ever provided a good explanation.

The Rocking Chair
and Other Cherokee Stories
A Retired Professor Shares Some Spooky Tales

It's one of those stories that have made the rounds year after year at Limestone College, circulating for decades. Supposedly, a young girl who died in the administration building in the mid-1800s never left. Upperclassmen will tell incoming freshman every year about the young girl's room and the ghostly tale of a rocking chair that sways with no wind. And according to a local historian and former Limestone professor, the chair does rock by itself—and he knows why.

But that is getting ahead of the story. According to Gaffney historian Bobby Moss, the tale started long before Limestone College even existed. A group of investors, including one of the past presidents of the University of South Carolina, decided to build a hotel in Gaffney in the mid-1830s to serve as a destination for the Lowcountry gentry who wanted to escape the hot summer months and mosquitoes that plagued them along the coast. The Upstate had become a destination spot, and especially Gaffney because of its natural springs. The Limestone Springs Hotel opened in 1835 and quickly gained a reputation as a nice place to stay.

The building still stands, in the center of the current Limestone College campus. Its long, white, Greek-style columns and round cupola give the building a rather distinguished and distinctive flare. But for various reasons the hotel's finances took a turn for the worse. It went bankrupt in 1845, but did not remain closed for long. An English encyclopedia salesman named Dr. Thomas Curtis bought the hotel with the idea of opening an all-girls' school that specialized in math and the sciences. The school did better than the hotel, but tragedy struck during the Civil War, and here is where the ghost story began that has haunted Limestone College ever since.

A student took ill and died while rocking in a chair in her room that overlooks the nearby limestone quarry which gives the school its name. It was a corner room on the top of the three-story building. Ever since then, any rocking chair placed in the room will rock all by itself at two separate times of the year.

The room soon gained a reputation for being haunted, and students refused to stay in it. Eventually the school expanded and became the present-day Limestone College, but students still refused to stay in the room. The old hotel became the school's administration building over time, which solved the problem of trying to get students to stay there. No students in the building equaled no students getting stuck with the haunted room.

Moss, who grew up in Gaffney, knew the legend of the rocking chair and took on an experiment when he was hired as a professor in the mid-1960s. Much to his surprise, he learned that the legend was true. A chair will rock all by itself at two separate points of the year, early spring and early fall.

He also learned the reason why it rocks. But he will not say what the truth is, vowing to keep the legend of the haunted room a tale worth repeating. He gave a hint, though, that somewhat adds to the legend. The rocking has to do with the tunnels that lead underneath the campus to the nearby quarry.

"I know what the truth is," he said. "But I don't want to spoil the fun."

The rocking chair isn't the only Cherokee County ghost story that Moss has investigated over the years. Cherokee is located between Spartanburg and the North Carolina border and seems to attract a fair number of ghosts, including one Moss vividly remembers seeing as a young man.

He said if motorists see a young woman late at night wearing a dress with blue flowers walking on Highway 5 near Kings Creek, just south of Blacksburg, they had better think twice before stopping to give her a ride. The young woman may not be what she appears. She may be the ghost of a young woman killed walking along the same road.

When drivers slow down to offer the woman a ride, she vanishes before they even stop the car. Several motorists have seen this young woman over the years. Her hair is dark and cut to the shoulder. While there are no reports about her face, her image is clear enough for people to see she is wearing high-laced shoes and a dress covered with small, blue periwinkle flowers. No one has actually seen her face, because she vanishes before motorists get a chance to take a second look. Moss said he saw the young woman back in the 1940s. As he turned to see who the woman was, she vanished in plain view.

Moss told a friend about seeing the woman one day. Wesley Love, who owned a country store in Kings Creek, overheard him telling the story and said he was not alone in seeing the apparition. Love told Moss and his friend that other people had also told him that they had seen the young woman. Moss later learned what may be the woman's tragic story. In 1928 a young woman walking along that portion of the road was accidentally shot and killed by her father. The girl's father didn't want her to go see her boyfriend. He was running behind the girl with a gun and was planning to shoot in the air to stop her. The gun slipped and he shot and killed his daughter.

"I saw her only once, in the late 1940s," Moss said. "I have tried to see her again, but you have to be in the right place at the right time."

During my research, I found several other stories that people share about Cherokee County. One of those tales pertains to Rock House Road, in Blacksburg. The road runs alongside the King's Mountain battleground. It got its name from a rock house that was constructed in the early 1800s. This house is still standing, and the ghost there can be viewed only one day a year. As the legend goes, the family that lived in the house had a mentally impaired daughter. Her father was embarrassed by her and forced her to stay locked up in a cellar during the day, but at night he would give her a candle and let her venture outside. One night the daughter decided to go out farther than usual. Then her candle blew out. The girl was lost. She tried to find her way in the darkness, but she was unsuccessful and died somewhere out in the wilderness just a few yards from home. The legend states that if you hold a lit candle to a car window along the road, the girl's face will appear as if drawn back to the light that extinguished the night she died.

A second Blacksburg ghost is reported along White Wolf Hollow, which lives up to its somewhat ominous name with a bevy of strange tales. People report seeing floating lights darting between trees. Hunters have reported running over "white monkeys" that cross the road in front of their trucks, but when they go back to look for them, there is nothing there. White Wolf Hollow is near King's Mountain park as well. The region, populated by numerous old cemeteries, is very isolated, and the road leading to the haunted area is very narrow and mostly gravel. It appears to never have been paved.

The Call in the Night
A Haunted House in West Pelzer

Rey McClain was stumbling around in the upstairs of his West Pelzer home when it happened. He was sleeping upstairs that night because a family friend was visiting his and his wife Kelly's recently renovated northern Anderson County home. The friend and Kelly had stayed up late to chat, so Rey had gone to sleep in the quieter second-floor front bedroom overlooking the immaculate front lawn.

It was late in the night when he went down the hall to use the bathroom. He was washing his hands when he heard a voice call out.

"Help me, help me, I'm dying."

It wasn't his wife's voice. Nor was it their friend's. A rush of fear mixed with adrenaline went over him. He crept to the edge of the stairs to see if something might be the matter, even though he was pretty sure he knew whom the voice belonged to. His suspicions were confirmed when his eyes scanned over the first-floor parlor. There was no one there. At least no one living was down there. The voice belonged to the spirit of Lulu Welborn, who had made her presence known as soon as the couple moved in.

Unlike many ghost stories, where rumors and legends merge fact and myth, the McClains' ghost is complete with backstory, numerous eyewitness accounts, and even a picture. Voices, sightings, and other oddities have been associated with the ghost of Lulu Welborn over the decades.

"We didn't talk about it for the longest time," McClain said. "We didn't want the attention, but now we are more open about it."

West Pelzer is located on the northeastern edge of Anderson County, along the banks of the Saluda River. Like its sister village of Pelzer, it is part of a string of small communities dotting the countryside. These are towns with loads of history and lore. Many current residents have ancestors who date back generations in the small towns, and many of their homes do too.

The McClains' house was built in 1893 by a local dry goods merchant named Walter Leland Welborn. His wife Lulu gave birth to eight children before she died in 1913 during an influenza epidemic. Welborn later remarried and added five more children to his brood. Decades later, some of those children still remembered hearing things in their home, such as strange voices and people calling their names when no one else was there.

The two-story house has a large rotunda-style porch and white siding. It is surrounded by trees and small shrubs, and the McClains have done everything they can to keep it looking the same as when the Welborn children played in the home. The house had a very interesting history after the Welborns left, but it is easy to see why the McClains decided not to decorate from that era. It became a funeral home in the early 1930s, with the present-day kitchen being used as an embalming room. The house was eventually sold and resold until it became the property of the town of West Pelzer. By the time the McClains bought the home in the early 1990s, it was almost completely falling in after being used as a storage facility for years. Another couple had tried to restore it, but stopped.

It only took a few weeks for the McClains to notice they were not alone in the house.

McClain, a pharmacist in Simpsonville, came home from work and walked into the kitchen. He tossed some items on a table and looked up a wall facing the kitchen door—a completely normal thing to do when entering a room. But what he saw in the mirror on the wall was not so natural.

He could clearly see a woman standing behind him. He spun around quickly, but no one was there. Although more than a little spooked by the incident, he decided to keep the story to himself. He feared that if he told his wife, she would want to move immediately.

A year went by and Rey McClain managed to keep his tale a secret. There were some unexplained events around the house, but no more sightings. They were renovating the house to get it back to its original look, and one of the jobs was installing an antique mantelpiece around the fireplace. The mantelpiece included a very large mirror. It was now time for Kelly McClain to see Lulu Welborn.

She was cleaning the mirror when she saw a woman sitting in a chair in the parlor. She had a natural reaction. She screamed. Rey McClain came running. He wasn't sure why, but he knew she must have seen the ghost.

His wife told him what had happened, but Rey wanted to make sure they had seen the same thing. Trying not to let on that he had seen the spirit a year before, Rey asked his wife what the woman looked like, suggesting details that were the opposite of what he had seen. Each time, she corrected him and gave answers that described exactly what he had witnessed. She had her hair pulled back and was wearing an off-yellow dress with a frilly, high-necked collar. She had a very solemn look. Sad, somber. Not scary.

It was then that he admitted he had seen the same woman. But by that time they knew they wanted to stay in the house. They would stay even if there was a ghost, which would soon get a name.

One of Walter Leland Welborn's sons dropped by one day. He was excited to see the old house being restored, and he brought along a book about the family's history. One of the pictures showed Lulu Welborn. It was the woman the husband and wife had seen. (They now have a picture of the dark-haired

Lulu saved on one of their computers.) The couple soon learned more about their spectral visitor, who they refer to as the lady or the spirit, and not as a ghost, including that she had died in the upstairs front bedroom where Rey McClain had been sleeping that night.

After the son's visit, the odd things began to multiply. The couple has a small set of photos taken by friends and guests that show something floating around the house and grounds. One clearly looks to be in the shape of a woman. Rey McClain said he has heard his name called out when no one else was around. Once they heard two men talking, but no one was there. The appearances happen most often when work is being done, which makes them believe renovation work stirs the spirits.

And things continued to get weirder.

Workers installing a pool in 2002 asked McClain if someone lived in the upstairs of the house after spotting a woman looking down at them several times during the day. McClain had a tough time explaining that one to them.

While Lulu has shown no aggression toward the family, the couple's various dogs have waged a small war with the spirit. One of their dogs, Ollie, would carry a rubber ball around in its mouth and bark at the stairs. One time the couple came home to find Ollie barking and the ball slowly bouncing down the stairs, step by step, as if thrown by someone. Other times they found the ball in places that the dog should not have been able to reach, such as on top of the refrigerator. Two more of their dogs, Charlise and Cooper, refuse to go upstairs, but will sit at the bottom and just bark upward.

Despite the little oddities, the McClains have no qualms living in a haunted house.

"We've come to accept this is part of the house," McClain said.

Devil on a Tombstone
One of the Upstate's Oldest Tales

Retired Limestone College professor Bobby Moss has been col-
lecting tales about the Upstate for decades. It's a natural thing
for him, considering he is also a Gaffney and Cherokee County
historian. One of the stories he knows involves the supernatural and dates back decades before even Limestone College was
founded. It revolves around a slave's fateful journey through a
rainstorm in the latter days of the 1700s.

The slave, Sam, was owned by a retired Continental officer
just after the end of the Revolutionary War. The officer's name
has been lost to history, but the colorfully creepy story of Sam
has lived on through the years. Sam and his master left their
Union County home one day for a fishing trip in York. The
master was going to see an old friend from the war, and their
goal was to catch some of the four hundred-pound sturgeon
swimming in Upstate rivers. The trip soon took a strange turn
when a slave came to York to tell Sam's master that his son had
taken ill. It was likely the boy was dying. Sam and the master
argued about whether to stay or leave. Night was coming quickly
and a storm was brewing in the east. They would have to cross
the Broad River, which would be swelled to the top with dark,
icy water if a storm hit. It was decided no storm could keep the
master from going home to his boy.

The two took off on their horses, with Sam in the lead, back
toward Union. Soon they were caught by the fierce storm. Sam
complained that he could not see because of the blinding rain

and dark sky, but the master told him to wrap his arms around the horse's neck. The animal knew the way home and would guide them. Sam clutched tightly, hoping the horse was heading the right way even though he doubted the animal could find the correct road.

Just then the horse stopped dead in its tracks. Sam was nearly thrown from the steed. He called back to the master to see what they should do, and the master called forward to say to wait until the next lightning flash and look around. They could get their bearings if the temporary flicker of light could illuminate the night sky long enough.

Sam waited as the rain spattered down on his head in buckets. His clothes stuck to him like a second skin. The lightning flashed. In an instant, Sam could see the horse's ears were up and its eyes were following the trail up a very long hill.

Sam didn't recognize the trail, but the master soon rode forward and urged both horses up the muddy hill just before the lightning flashed again. Sam was able to look to both sides of him during the momentary burst of light. He saw crooked headstones and wrought-iron fences. Old crosses marked the edge of the nearby trail. They were in a graveyard. Sam and the master were definitely off their trail. The master told Sam to get down and look to see where the new trail led. Sam refused. The master chided him for being scared, and said he would dismount and look to see if the trail led out of the cemetery. Sam wasn't too keen on that idea either. He didn't want to be left alone guarding the horses during a storm, in an area he didn't recognize—and especially in a graveyard that seemed to pop up out of nowhere.

They sat for a few seconds staring at each other and decided to both go. The lightning flashed right as they dismounted, and Sam and the master saw a freshly filled grave just ahead. Sam stepped back a few feet. He felt in the bottom of his stomach that this was why the horse was scared. Something was strangely wrong with the grave. If Sam thought he had been scared before, this was much worse. The lightning flashed again. Sam saw there was a hole in the ground just about where the head should have been. The slave and the master both stood there shaking as the cold rain pummeled them. Just then the noise of the rain subsided and they could hear something growling in the grave.

The master told Sam to stick his hand down the hole to see what it was. Sam, of course, refused and told the master to stick his hand down the hole. The master just smiled back and thrust his hand into the hole.

One can only imagine the master's and Sam's expressions at what happened next. The master said he found something with hair on it. It must be a dead body. Just then, though, the hair started to move and the master grabbed on tight. Whatever was down in the hole was kicking up a fit, and the master held on with all of his might as his arm moved up and down out of the hole like a bilge pump on a boat.

With a final tug, the master ripped his arm from the hole. There in his hands was an opossum. Its shiny black hair glistened in the rain. The master threw the animal on the tombstone and walked back to the horses with a step of confidence. Sam followed silently. As they rode off, though, Sam craned his head back one more time at the tombstone. The opossum was no longer there.

Instead, sitting on the tombstone basked in an eerie light was a devil with two horns sticking out of its forehead. The devil just sat there laughing as he watched Sam and the master ride away back down the trail.

The rest of their travel was less frightful, and eventually they made it home to Union, where the master's son survived his illness. Sam, of course, told people about the trip and what he had seen perched on the tombstone. The master also told the tale, but with one important change. He never saw a devil on the tombstone. It was just a squirming opossum trying to figure out what had just happened when the master looked back.

But Sam always had an explanation for the difference in the ending. The master was just too scared to admit what he had seen.

The Hound of Goshen
A Ghostly Hound and Other Tales
from Newberry County

Old Buncombe Road was once one of the busiest roads in the state, with stage coaches filled with Lowcountry travelers making their way north during the humid summer months. The road runs parallel to what is now Interstate 26, and in a way that highway keeps on the tradition of ferrying passengers up and down the state. However, I-26 doesn't have a ghost story quite like the Hound of Goshen. Newberry historian James Clamp said the story of the Hound of Goshen is one of the most repeated and most varied ghost stories in the county.

"Whether it is true or not, I just don't know," he said.

There are several versions involving the five-mile stretch of road between old Ebenezer Church, located in the Maybinton Township, and Goshen Hill in Union County. Around 1850, a peddler and his faithful dog passed through the settlement about the time a gruesome murder occurred, so one version of the legend goes. Being a stranger, the peddler had no one to stand up for his integrity, and after a hasty "trial" he was publicly hanged. His poor, white hound dog stayed beside his master during the hanging, and for three days after the dead man was buried the dog stayed at the spot and howled pitifully. The annoyed people in the community put an end to this by stoning the poor animal to death. It wasn't very long until travelers along the old road began reporting a large, white dog that would lurch at their horses as they rode by the church's cemetery late at night.

The fierce hound was described as being ghostly white and having red eyes and large fangs. The animal would scare the horses so badly they would not slow down until they reached Goshen Hill a few miles away. Many remembered the poor peddler killed there and believed it was his dog back from the grave still trying to avenge his beloved master.

One variation of the tale states that those brave enough to confront the snarling beast would slash at the dog with their buggy whips, which invariably passed through the apparition as if trying to cut fog. The dog would follow the frightened passengers until it reached a certain cemetery—then was seen to leap through the locked gates.

Others, though, were not scared by the animal. A country physician kept a home on the old road, and until his death he maintained that the ghost dog often accompanied him on his rounds—he was never afraid of the ghost and considered it to be a friend. The ghost dog was often reported to be spotted near the doctor's home.

The decades passed and the road was paved. Automobiles replaced the horse and buggy, but the dog was still reportedly seen by those in cars, on horseback, and others out for an evening stroll. One night in 1936 a young man was frightened almost to death by the dog, and barely reached his doctor's house before passing out. The dog was reported in the late 1970s by an old lady sitting on her porch, which faced the road. She claimed a large, white dog came into her yard, increased in size, and leapt toward her. She fainted dead away, but was able to recount her story when she recovered.

However, the origin of the story, like most ghost tales, has some variations as well. A second popular version states that the peddler was robbed of the little money he had and murdered. The man's white hound dog was known to accompany him everywhere he went, but was absent when the man died. The local community members buried the man, and they later found the dead dog lying across the man's grave. In this version, a larger-than-average white hound has been seen hundreds of times in hot pursuit of travelers, though in this case people believe the dog is trying to protect his owner rather than avenge him.

Clamp noted that the ghost dog has been spoken about for years, but he said he hasn't heard anything about a new sighting in quite some time.

However, he did have one very disturbing tale to add to the list of Newberry ghosts. The story starts with old Kadesh Methodist Church, which was active in the 1820s in Newberry. It closed, though, in the 1830s when its congregation merged with another church to form Trinity United Methodist. The former Kadesh building was kept in use by people in the community wanting to celebrate a wedding or hold a funeral without the horse and buggy ride to Trinity. At one point in the 1850s, friends of an elderly woman found what they believed was her dead body. Shaken by the woman's death, they decided to hold a funeral in the morning at Kadesh and transported her there in a coffin. In the middle of the service, though, the woman sat upright in the coffin, looked around, and asked loudly, "What are you people doing here?"

As can be expected, people ran for the doors, thinking the woman had somehow returned from the dead, Clamp said. It turns out she was just a heavy sleeper. Apparently she didn't breathe as deeply as she slept.

Being buried alive wasn't unheard of, he said. Because there were no embalming fluids, the "dead" were often buried very quickly to make sure the body didn't start to decompose. This led to a lot of people getting buried without a truly reliable determination of whether they were dead or not.

During my investigations into Newberry ghosts, I unearthed a couple of other tales that Clamp couldn't confirm, but they are worth mentioning. One involves a place called Flag Lake, which is not really a lake, but rather more of a crater where one was once supposed to be built. The legend states the construction workers must have been scared off. On the hill there is a cemetery with a long row of gravestones that all say the

92

people committed suicide. Some locals have reported having trouble starting their vehicles while parked near the cemetery.

Another tale involves old West End Cemetery, where on certain nights people have claimed to have seen the dreary form of a lady in a wedding dress. She's been spotted sitting in the trees, standing by her grave, and roaming the fields next to the cemetery. She is said to be waiting for her lover to come and take her to their wedding.

The Lady in White
A Ghost Story Worth Sharing

Wes and Peggy Lawton didn't want to sell their house in northern Greenville County. They had put so much effort into restoring it. But the repair work was becoming so much of a hassle that in 1983 they decided to sell the stately manor that had been built by Wes's great-grandparents and which was known in the family for the distinctive boulders that sat out front. They left the new owners—distant cousins of Wes's—all the furniture and a bottle of champagne to celebrate the new home.

Peggy said it was so tough to sell that they refused to go back for almost seven years to even see the house. However, seven years is a long time, and curiosity started to get the better of them. They called the new owners and were invited to come by for dinner.

The Lawtons said sure, expecting a nice southern-style meal, with southern hospitality included. They expected a long night of telling old family stories. It was not to be, Peggy Lawton said.

"As soon as we got there they sat us down in the living room and started fussing at us," she recalled years later.

The new family wanted to know why the Lawtons hadn't told them about the "visitor in white." Peggy and Wes shook their heads. They had no idea what the family was talking about. The couple prompted Peggy and Wes, "You know, the woman in white who comes downs the steps." Peggy and Wes were still not sure until the woman said bluntly, "Why didn't you tell us about the ghost?"

94

A ghost? They had never seen a ghost in their fifteen years there, Peggy answered. Surely, they were joking. The couple shook their heads this time and began to tell a chilling story.

One day shortly after they moved into the house, the new couple's grandson came tearing into the kitchen saying he saw a woman in white coming down the stairs. The child was very distressed by what he thought was an intruder in the home. The family checked the room and the house, but found no one. They chalked it up to the child's imagination even though he was highly agitated by what he had seen. But not long afterward, the fiancée of one of their children reported seeing a woman in white descending the stairs. The description matched the child's almost exactly.

Wes and Peggy apologized, but said they had never had a problem of any kind with any spectral visitors. After the evening, they asked their own children if they had ever seen anything. The children, who by now were adults, said no, but they said they always felt the house was spooky to be in.

In looking at the house's history, Peggy decided only one person in the house's past matched the description. The home had been built in 1902 by Wes's great-grandfather, John F. Wyman, a doctor from Aiken, to use as a summer home. As part of the construction, John Wyman's wife, Rosemond Hack Wyman, hand carved the rods in the stairwell.

"Her handprints are practically all over the house," Peggy said.

And Rosemond Wyman was known to wear all white almost all the time. A woman in white on Rosemond Wyman's hand-carved staircase? Peggy doesn't think it is a coincidence. She surmised that when they sold the house out of the direct family, Rosemond Wyman wanted to see who the new people were. She must have been calmed when she learned the family was not a threat to the house she adored so much while alive.

"She never bothered anyone," Peggy Lawton said. "I think she was just curious and wanted people to know she was still around and cared."

Something Afoot at the Walnut Grove Plantation
What Really Happened in the Weeks Leading Up to the Battle of Cowpens?

One of the Upstate's oldest ghost stories dates back to the American Revolution, when the Upstate was a hotly contested battleground between loyalists to the British Crown and the Carolinians wanting to break away. It's a ghost story that involves spies, a possible murder, mysterious stains on the floor, and a two centuries-old debate about what really happened at the Walnut Grove Plantation. Many legends exist, but the truths behind the tales are sometimes more exciting than the myths.

Walnut Grove Plantation today looks remarkably similar to how it did more than 225 years ago, when the events that triggered the ghost story took place, said Becky Slayton, the site's administrator. King George III granted 550 acres to Charles Moore in 1763, when the area around Spartanburg was the backcountry, instead of being the urban area it is now, Slayton said. The house was built in 1765 with two rooms and a closet on the bottom floor and another room upstairs. Charles Moore and his wife, Mary, closed in a back porch and split the upstairs into three rooms before they died in 1805. They had good reason to add to the house. They had ten children.

The main two-story house has double-shouldered chimneys, clapboard-over-log construction, and Queen Anne mantles. It remained in the Moore family for more than 150 years, but was used mostly by tenant farmers after the couple's death. It was purchased in 1961 to be converted into a historic site, which it has been ever since. The building's roof, siding, and first floor were replaced, but everything from the pine supports to the second story's floor remains intact, which is an important part of the legend.

The property is full of furniture and other antiques collected throughout the years to capture pre-1805 Spartanburg life. The house and surrounding historic site are located in the Roebuck community, which is in the southern section of Spartanburg County, just off Interstate 26 and not far from the Dorman High School campus. The grounds also include Rocky Spring Academy, a separate kitchen, a blacksmith's forge, a wheat house, a smoke house, a barn, a well house, and Dr. Andrew Barry Moore's office, according to Walnut Grove's website.

Numerous towering oak trees surround the home, along with several herb gardens. The Moore family cemetery is also located on the grounds. Numerous family members, soldiers, and slaves are buried there. Revolutionary War heroine Margaret Katherine Barry is among the interred. It is probably one of the county's prettiest spots as well one of the area's biggest tourism attractions.

It is also the home of Festifall, a family oriented, two-day event centered on the reenactments of life on a pre-Revolutionary Upstate colonial plantation, held every October. Among the attractions are demonstrations of colonial life, storytelling, a reenactment of "Bloody Bill" Cunningham's raid on Walnut Grove Plantation, militia drills, musket firing, eighteenth-century dancing, and colonial-era music.

It is Cunningham's raid that has sparked the main haunting rumors. The Moores were major proponents of independence from the British, and Walnut Grove was a recruiting station for the American Patriots, Slayton said. "Bloody Bill" Cunningham had deserted from the American side and was leading a group of Tory soldiers to burn down the Moores' home in 1780, just a few months before the fateful Battle of

97

Cowpens. It was part of an overall campaign to root out Upstate rebels.

The main legend states that a Patriot officer, possibly Captain Ben Steadman, took refuge at Walnut Grove when he became ill or was wounded in battle. It is said Cunningham killed Steadman in an upstairs bedroom. Two other soldiers with Steadman were killed at the cemetery nearby. Over the years, both guests and employees have reported seeing Steadman's ghost in the house and on the grounds. The eeriest part of the story, though, is the legend that Steadman's bloodstains still mark the spot where he was slain.

Slayton, though, said there are a lot of mysteries about what happened. It is more likely Steadman was killed in the skirmish, but whether he died in or out of the house is debated. She also added Steadman was probably not killed in cold blood, as the legend goes.

As for the supposed blood spots, well, they're not really blood. But no one is quite sure what the dark brown spots on the upstairs bedroom floor are. There are several of them, though. Most are no bigger than a quarter, but several others are five or six inches wide. It is highly possible the stains came during the many years the house was used by tenant farmers.

However, the second part of the ghost story involves one of the Moores' ten children, Margaret Katherine Barry, who was married to a Revolutionary War officer named Andrew Barry. One account has Mrs. Barry, who was known as Kate, riding on horseback from Walnut Grove to warn General Daniel Morgan about advancing British forces. She knew that the soldiers from her husband's militia unit had all returned to their farms and that all available men would be desperately needed to halt the enemy's advance. Morgan is said to have used her information to rally his men. His January 1781 engagement at the Battle of Cowpens routed the British troops and was a major victory in the war. Less than ten months later, the American forces would defeat the British at Yorktown and effectively end the conflict.

"Because she was a woman she was able to travel somewhat freely and tell Patriot forces about British troop movements," Slayton said.

The spirit of a young woman is often seen walking near the house by employees and visitors, and the legend states it is Kate Barry still protecting her home. Slayton doesn't believe the story because Kate Barry did not die at Walnut Grove. She sees no reason for her to be there. For the record, she doesn't believe any of the ghost tales.

However, Barry's ride is of some historical note. The Franklin Mint commemorated Barry with a 44 millimeter-wide pewter medal in 1975 as part of its "Great Women of the American Revolution" series. The front shows a woman with her cape blowing in the wind riding a horse across knee-deep water. The back includes her name and the words "She became the heroine of the Battle of Cowpens by volunteering as a scout for the patriots of South Carolina. Her mission assured an important American victory." If it there is a female ghost haunting Walnut Grove, who better than a woman who did so much to spread freedom.

Shadows and Voices
Strange Things in a Downtown Greenville Office

It was early winter and the sun was just setting. Bill Bishop and Joel Hogg's printing company, emedia group, had moved into new offices in downtown Greenville in the last few weeks, and the two co-owners were the only ones there after several long days of getting things organized. Bishop was sitting in his office and had an old turntable playing very quietly in the background as he looked over some files. Out of nowhere, he heard a scratchy voice whisper: "Bill, Bill."

"It was like somebody had shot something through me, I turned around so fast," Bishop recalled.

He looked toward the open door at the other end of his office. No one was there. He picked up the phone, thinking somebody—maybe Hogg—had figured out the new intercom system.

Nothing.

He looked at the stereo.

Still nothing.

Somebody had to be playing a trick on him, so he eased away from his desk and walked quietly to his door. He jumped through the doorway to surprise anyone hiding behind the corner, but instead found himself standing in the dark hallway alone. He looked up and down, but no one else was there. He crept along the wooden floors toward Hogg's office with the thought that his normally stoic business partner was playing a trick. Bishop peeked into the office to see Hogg busy at work with his head down. Bishop watched for a good minute to see if Hogg was going to get back up and play another trick.

Hogg just kept his head down and continued working, so Bishop finally walked in. Hogg looked up, saw his distraught friend's face, and asked what was the matter. Bishop, who is normally very jovial, said very directly, "Please tell me you did that." Hogg stared back. His face showed no trace of knowing what Bishop was talking about.

"That was pretty strange," Bishop recalled.

It wouldn't be the last strange thing that happened.

Emedia's offices are located in a downtown building that once served as a funeral home before becoming a successfull printing company for close to eighty years. When Hogg and Bishop bought the company in 2004, several of the old-timers working in the basement said there was a ghost in the building, but they didn't elaborate.

Two emedia employees soon told them another strange tale, not long after the night that Bishop had heard the voice in his office. The man and woman had been working in her office, and the woman was goofing around and singing the high part to the song "Loving You." The man asked her to stop, saying her voice was killing him. She complied and they both left the office for a few minutes. He came back first and heard the same song playing on his coworker's computer. He was annoyed, but not angry. He thought she was messing around with him by putting the CD in. She came back, and he asked her about the song. She said she hadn't done anything and tapped the little button to release the CD drawer.

She popped a shiny Rod Stewart CD out, and then showed her coworker that she hadn't been playing the song off the Internet either.

Bishop said other employees started to see a strange shadow, especially in the kitchen area. The shadow was hard to explain. It looked like it came from a person, but that was impossible because no one was walking by. Bishop described it as something you saw out of the corner of your eye. You knew it was there, but you could never turn fast enough to get a good look at it. They also heard loud thumping noises that couldn't be explained.

Finally, Bishop was in his office with another employee when they heard a loud, garbled noise that sounded like a few seconds of music being played backward. Before either person could get up, they heard the noise again. Bishop and Hogg were stumped as to what might have been causing the noises until Bishop's young daughter found a framed picture in one of the closets. It was of the original owner of the printing company. The little girl guessed he was the ghost and that he was making the noises because he felt he was no longer needed or appreciated. So Bishop dusted off the picture and put the black-and-white photo on his desk with pictures of his family.

"It's kind odd, because there in the middle of all my kids is a picture of an old man."

But it ended the strange rumblings, so there it will stay.

Haunted Bridges
Young Women and Bridges Don't Mix Well Here

Charles Brookover almost sounded bored as he related the story of Cry Baby bridge in Union County, he has told it so many times to people inquiring about the legend. On the way to Rose Hill Plantation is an old bridge with a rusted steel frame. It has gained infamy for a ghastly tale dating back to 1950, when a woman threw her young child over the side of the bridge into the waters below. The only reason given was that she wanted to spite her husband. As the story goes, the woman's spirit now comes back at night looking for her child. The legend passed on by students at area high schools is that if someone parks on the bridge and cuts off their engine's motor, they will hear a baby crying and see the mother looking for it. Brookover has worked at the historic Rose Hill Plantation for years and drolly reports that he has never seen or heard anything from the bridge. However, he also admits he has never gone looking for anything, either.

The plantation offers a look at antebellum South Carolina, surrounded by trees and manicured lawns. It is also the historic home of South Carolina's "Secession Governor," William H. Gist. Rose Hill has been restored over the years to reflect Gist's era. That includes antique furnishings and memorabilia. Gardens, trails, and towering trees provide a backdrop to the mansion, which is listed on the National Register of Historic Places. However, the plantation has no real connection to the ghost story other than being a location marker to the tale, but Brookover will tell the story if you ask about it.

Martin Meek, a local architect and historian, gave another theory about the bridge. He said an epidemic around the 1830s killed a large number of children and that some were buried in a cemetery not too far from the bridge. He visited the cemetery years ago and felt there was something not quite right about the little graveyard.

Meek said Union's Cry Baby bridge isn't the only overpass with a ghostly tale involving a young woman. There is also Granny Nesbitt's bridge, which crosses the Tyger just below the river's headwaters in Spartanburg County. It is said some motorists driving along the road will see a young woman trying to flag them down at the bridge. The young woman will get in the car, he said, and ask the driver to take her down the road a little bit. She will invariably vanish before they reach their destination. The legend doesn't say who the woman is or why her ghost haunts the road. The bridge is named, oddly enough, after an old woman who lived along the road in a house facing the span, but she is not attached to the ghost tale.

A second ghostly bridge in Spartanburg involves two fishermen whose ghosts still relive their final few minutes. The bridge, located off of Highway 56 about halfway between the city of Spartanburg and the Union County line, is a popular spot for ghost watchers. According to the tale I heard, two fishermen were killed by some kind of beast with glowing red eyes that lived underneath the bridge. It is said that if you wait on top of the bridge late at night, you can hear two men's voices as they laugh and have a good time, their boots sloshing through the water. Then, out of nowhere, people have claimed to hear their screams as something attacks them. Witnesses claim to have seen a pair of red glowing eyes along the bank when this happens. One person told me she and her friends went there once while in college after hearing the story from students at Spartanburg High School. She claimed to have heard the voices, but she hightailed it out of there before waiting to look for a pair of red eyes.

And Union's Cry Baby bridge isn't the only bridge to carry that odd name. There is a small, poorly paved, double-lane road over Rock Creek just along the banks of Lake Hartwell, in Anderson County. Along its course you will find a set of double bridges. One is the current road, while the second, rusted-out, kudzu-covered bridge is on an abandoned parallel road. The legend states that a woman and her child died under the abandoned bridge. At night people claim to have seen a woman wearing a white dress walking near the bridge, while others say they have heard the unexplained sound of a crying baby.

Another haunted bridge is in northeastern Anderson County, on Three Bridges Road in the Powdersville community. The origins of the tale are somewhat murky, but it states that a young black girl, possibly a slave named Eloise, committed suicide along one of the three bridges that give the road its name. As the story goes, Union soldiers killed the girl's master as they traveled through Powdersville on their way to battle, and that is why she killed herself. It is said her spirit still haunts the road and that people have heard her scream. The road starts behind Mt. Airy Baptist Church and runs almost all the way through to Highway 153. It is a fairly winding road with not a lot of houses, and no one on the road could confirm the legend. It should be noted that it is unlikely Union soldiers ever went through Powdersville, which is said to have gotten its name because it was a Confederate weapons depot.

One final bridge of note is Seven Devils Bridge in Woodruff, which is located in lower Spartanburg County. People have said this spooky old bridge cannot be crossed at the stroke of midnight. The bridge is no longer drivable, as the roads nearby have long since been abandoned and the very old bridge over a small, unnamed stream can only be found by foot. However, the legend does not explain why a person cannot cross the bridge at midnight or how it got such a sinister moniker.

Who's There?
And Some Scary Answers at the Walnut Lane Inn

David Ades was preparing the upstairs of the Walnut Lane Inn for some evening guests when he heard someone yell up to him, "They're here." Ades figured it was his business partner, Hoyt Dottry, calling up the arrival and thought nothing of it. He figured Dottry would let the guests in and he could continue his tasks. That is, until the doorbell rang.

Wondering what was going on, Ades went downstairs and found the guests standing outside the large wooden doors leading into the 100-plus-year-old house just on the outskirts of downtown Lyman.

He greeted them, sat them down, and then went to find Dottry to see why he had told him the guests had arrived but then left them standing on the front wraparound porch. Ades found Dottry coming in from the workshop behind the bed and breakfast. Dottry said he had been out back and was just coming up because he figured their friends would have arrived by now. He hadn't been inside a few minutes before and he certainly hadn't announced their arrival.

Ades just grumbled to himself. It was another encounter with the ghosts at the Walnut Lane Inn. Dottry will talk about the stories, but admits he doesn't like the idea of the place being haunted. Ades just doesn't discuss it.

"David doesn't like talking about what happens," Dottry explained. "I don't like it either, but it's there. Luckily they are peaceful ghosts. I think they are happy with what we've done."

Among the ghosts believed to roam the gorgeous antebellum mansion are the original builder, A.G. Groce, his two daughters, and at least one maid. There may be more. Numerous guests have asked about what kinds of spooks might be hiding there, after experiencing strange noises at night.

During daylight hours, the Walnut Lane Inn is hardly the place that would seem to be the stuff of spooky nightmares. It is located a few blocks from downtown Lyman, but it seems so far away from everything. That's because it is partially secluded from view by a row of trees and sits on a small hill. The house has been renovated with new siding over the years, but its green shutters and old brick chimney keep much of the structure's original charm. It is a popular spot for weddings, and the grounds surrounding the distinguished building are filled with flower gardens and magnolia trees.

The house was built in 1902 by Groce, a prominent area businessman, and was considered one of Spartanburg County's largest homes at one time. The Groce family sold the home in 1995 to a couple who wanted to make it into a bed and breakfast. Dottry and Ades, who were from Florida, bought the building from them in 2000 because they were looking for a new business venture. The little town of Lyman and the old home seemed like the perfect spot to set up shop—even if they had some reservations. Dottry specifically asked if the place was haunted. He didn't have any particular feeling coming in, such as that someone was watching him. He just wanted to know. He was assured it was spook free.

"I don't deal well with that sort of thing," he said. "I kept asking if the place was haunted."

However, the story changed no sooner than the ink dried on the sales deal. One of the former owners fessed up to some unusual events, such as hearing her name called when no one else was around. It didn't take long for Dottry and Ades to figure out there was more than just name calling.

They went about a redecoration process—mostly painting and new wallpaper. But one of the bigger chores was replacing the chandelier in the main parlor area. Dottry turned off the power and tested the electricity twice before starting work. The circuit was dead, so he went to fetch the chandelier that is now the centerpiece to the comfy room. He soon returned, and when he got to the top of the ladder, the old light came on just before he started to unscrew it.

With his head almost nine feet off the ground, his first though was that Ades had switched the power on. Ades, though, came in to say he hadn't done a thing. Remembering the story from the former owner, Dottry made an impassioned plea—he and Ades were trying to make the house better. They weren't out to destroy it. That seemed to appease the ghosts' decorative curiosities, but it didn't stop them from letting themselves be known around the house.

A few months later, Dottry was in the kitchen around 9 P.M. preparing coffee for the next morning's breakfast. As he readied a pot, he caught a glimpse of something in the corner of his eye. It was a man standing around 5 foot 6 and wearing a dark suit. Dottry's brain registered the clothes as being of an older style, maybe dating back to the 1920s. As he turned to see who was standing just a few feet away, the figure disappeared.

"It seemed like it lasted thirty years, but it was only just a few seconds," he said. "All I know is I saw it and the next thing I knew I was out the door."

Dottry soon learned the identity of his spectral visitor when a relative of the original owners came to see him with pictures of how the house once looked and snapshots of some of the previous residents. As Dottry rummaged through the stack of black and white photos from a bygone age, he found a picture of A.G. Groce. He was wearing a dark suit—the same exact clothes as were worn by the visitor in the kitchen.

"I didn't say anything to them," Dottry said. "My jaw just dropped."

It should be noted that this was one of the few times I ever felt something myself. As Dottry explained this story to me, I had the uneasy feeling that someone was right over my shoulder. I turned my head around several times to see if someone was there, but all that stood there was a piano against the parlor wall. I can't explain it, but I actually got cold chills. I didn't tell Dottry about what happened, because I didn't want to spook him any further.

The strange goings-on keep occurring for Dottry and his guests. It was shortly after the sighting in the kitchen that guests and passersby began to tell him stories. A woman attending a wedding on the inn's grounds told him the ghost of an old maid was in the kitchen and that she often watched people do the dishes. Others would later tell him the same thing.

Another guest, a psychic, told him there were ghosts of two young women who frequented the inn. Dottry was somewhat incredulous at first and asked the woman for more details. He figured she might be kidding him or had heard the story about their ghosts from other people. He pretended not to know what she was referring to. The patron then told in great detail about two young women whose presence was strong in the front parlor. Dottry knew he had to come clean with the guest, because he had heard the women's ghostly whispers on numerous occasions. It was normally when he was working in his office late at night.

"It's just some mindless chatter. I can't hear what they say, but it's like they are gossiping," he said. "They are snickering to themselves like they are sharing an old story or talking about a boyfriend."

The first time he heard the nocturnal whispers, he crept toward the parlor to see who was there because no one was staying at the inn at the time. He was a little shocked to find no one there. It has happened enough times now that he no longer checks.

It is possible the spirits are Groce's daughters, who inherited the home after he died. Neither was willing to sell, so they split the house to accommodate each other. Could it be they are split no more? Based on the late-night conversations in the front parlor, maybe so. Dottry said he is fine if they keep talking to each other. He just doesn't want them chatting with him.

The Ghost of Theodosia Burr Alston
One of South Carolina's Most Famous Ghosts Has Greenville Ties

The house just doesn't fit in. It is two stories high with a larger-than-average piece of land around it compared to the rest of the neighborhood. The other houses are ranch-style or trailers, and most sit on lots barely bigger than their homes. This one has a wraparound porch with white handrails on the bottom and a large balcony up top that juts out of the second floor. It has a tool shed full of nineteenth-century mill equipment out back. It has fireplaces in almost every room. While the rest of the houses around it appear to have been built in the 1950s, this one dates back a century earlier. And in fact, its faded-brick foundation dates back to the earliest days of the 1800s.

If that was not enough to make the place stand out, it has one more little interesting piece of history. It is rumored to be haunted. But not by just any ghost. It is the ghost of Theodosia Burr Alston, the daughter of a vice president of the United States and the wife of a South Carolina governor. Her mysterious 1812 disappearance at sea is one of the most talked about legends in state history.

Theodosia Burr Alston was somewhat of an anomaly for her time. She was highly educated and taught to be free-thinking, according to the acclaimed biography of her by Richard Cote. Her father was a prominent lawyer from Albany, New York, named Aaron Burr, a rising political figure who would loom large over his daughter's life. She was born in 1783 in

Albany, but spent most of her early years living on a New York City estate with her father, who first gained fame as a member of General George Washington's inner cadre of advisors during the Revolutionary War. Her mother died when Theodosia was very young.

Burr proved an adoring but demanding father to her. He recognized her intelligence and had her learn Latin, French, German, and Greek by the age of twelve. She could speak all four fluently. Burr envisioned a grand life for his daughter in hopes she would serve as a model for later generations. Cote's book states every moment of her day was directed and shaped by her father's vision.

"He was not interested in turning out just a smart, pretty girl; a father's pride; or a husband's delight. Burr was no petty theorist. He was a passionate, egotistical visionary on scale that made the gods cringe. With his vision and his daughter's talent, Burr intended to push the envelope of mortal achievement to its absolute limit. Burr's goal was to sculpt Theodosia into a model for the woman of the future: a female Aaron Burr," according to Cote.

"She was not trained to serve hearth, home, or plantation. From her first breath of life, she was groomed and educated to take her intended station in life: nothing less than president, queen . . . or empress."

However, the plan got sidetracked somewhat when Theodosia met a wealthy, charismatic South Carolina rice planter named Joseph Alston. They were married in 1801 and became the first recorded newlyweds to visit Niagara Falls. They split time between her father's New York estate and Alston's ancestral home on the Waccamaw River along the South Carolina coast. For all purposes, it was a happy union, and a son, Aaron Burr Alston, was born in Charleston in 1802. Yet, her loyalties were torn between her new family and her ever-demanding father.

Despite being a confidant of Washington and a war hero, her father is somewhat of an enigma over Theodosia's life and

U.S. history. His later exploits include a bitter loss to Thomas Jefferson in the presidential election of 1800. Each had received the same number of electoral votes, but Congress appointed Jefferson the third president of the United States. Burr was relegated to vice president under the election laws of the day. He bitterly accepted, but gained more infamy in 1804 when he dueled political arch rival Alexander Hamilton, another former Washington aide. Both men could have called off the duel, but Hamilton ended up dying due to his wounds. Hamilton's political legacy was elevated because of his early death.

Aaron Burr's life went in another direction. He formulated a bizarre plan to get residents in southwestern states to secede from the Union and become part of Mexico, where Burr would become emperor and Theodosia would be empress.

Theodosia and her husband were the financial backers of the "Mexican Conspiracy." Such a plan couldn't be kept secret, and President Jefferson soon learned of the scheme. Burr was tried but acquitted of treason. Still, the damage was done to his career. Burr exiled himself to Europe for four years—growing more impoverished as time passed.

Theodosia's life was also becoming increasingly difficult. The birth of her child left her with a host of medical problems. She was so convinced she was about to die that she wrote a farewell letter to her husband in 1805. She didn't die, but spent time living in Greenville between 1807 and 1810, according to local history. Greenville was emerging as a resort area at this time, and the Alstons spent time at the Prospect Hill home of one of Joseph's distant cousins, where the Greenville Water System's headquarters are now located. A neighbor there was Vardry McBee, the founder of modern Greenville.

Theodosia enjoyed Greenville enough that she convinced her husband to build a home there as well. There are few details left about what the house looked like, but records show it was built in what would become the Woodside community. The house would eventually burn down in 1857, but a new house was built on the Alstons' foundation in a matter of months.

Despite her failing health, Theodosia lived long enough to be reunited briefly with her father in 1812. The joyous event was short-lived, for a month later her son died from malaria. She desperately wished to return to New York to see her father again, but there were two interrelated problems facing the voyage. First, the young American republic was at war with Great Britain. British warships controlled the waters up and down the Atlantic seaboard, making ocean travel perilous. Second, Joseph Alston had just been elected South Carolina's governor and could not leave the state because he was the head of the militia. Theodosia, though, had been reared to think for herself and decided to make the trip anyway. She, a physician, and servants boarded a former privateer called *The Patriot* on New Year's Eve 1812. She was never seen alive again. The emphasis is on the alive.

No one is quite sure what became of Theodosia's voyage. It is possible the boat sank in a storm. One tale said pirates captured the ship and she was forced to walk the plank and quickly drowned. Another legend states Theodosia was found on the beach on the Outer Banks of North Carolina in a bedraggled state. It has been rumored an unsigned, undated painting known as the "Nag's Head portrait" that was discovered on the Outer Banks in 1869 is the final portrait of Theodosia. From there, her tale is unknown.

But there are many ghost stories from up and down the coast. On foggy nights, people who stand on the beach at Huntington Beach State Park have claimed to see the slender figure of Theodosia suspended above the water. Is she still walking the plank or looking for her former home by the seas?

Cape Hatteras in North Carolina also reports sightings. Not long after the disappearance of *The Patriot,* fishermen there claimed to see the figure of a young woman along the beach on moonlit nights. Some thought she was the ghost of a poor fisherman's daughter who had died shortly before her marriage. But others said it was the ghost of the beautiful Theodosia waiting for a ship to take her back to her grieving husband.

The story in Greenville is that Theodosia's ghost returned to her home overlooking Woodside, where she stayed for years, even after it burned down. The most consistent report is that people have felt a sad presence inside the home and heard the gentle rustling of a skirt flitting down the hallways. Residents in the nearby community report a lot of strange activity inside the house. But unfortunately, it is usually just vagrants and young teens who have broken into the abandoned home. A family had been restoring the house and even put new siding and a roof on the structure, but they stopped one day. The house was later repossessed by a bank. Numerous windows have been smashed and at least two doors have been kicked in. Several of the plaster walls inside have large holes knocked in them. White curtains left in the window blow lazily in the breeze. If Theodosia Burr Alston is still haunting the home, no one is there to see it.

Odds and Ends to Raise One Last Chill

Some ghost stories are just simple and short. I found many while researching this book that can be summed up in just a few hundred words. Here are some of the better ones.

Like Mother, Like Daughter?

Joe and Dianna Hiltabidel were driving through downtown Simpsonville one day when their daughter, who was then almost three, asked what the little boy walking along the railroad tracks was carrying. The couple turned to look and see what the inquisitive youngster was looking at. But there was nothing there.

Dianna asked her daughter, Sadie, if the boy was still there, thinking whomever she had seen must have jumped from the railroad tracks that split the downtown. Sadie answered that the boy was holding something, but she didn't know what it was. The couple tried to get the girl to explain what he was wearing, but she was too young to give a description. The signal light changed and they drove on, with Sadie still talking about the boy.

The work of an overactive imagination? An optical illusion? Dianna Hiltabidel doesn't think so.

"I am convinced that children can see something that adults can't," she said.

Hiltabidel may have some experience in what children see. When she was around five years old, she was playing in the living room of her grandmother's home in North Carolina. It

115

was a really old house and she looked up to see someone standing in the doorway to the kitchen. It was a very tall, thin man in a black suit and tie.

"I remember seeing him and not saying anything. He was just looking down. Then all of a sudden he just wasn't there," she said.

The apparition locked in her young brain, and years later she was looking through an old family photo album. On one of the pages was the picture of a tall man wearing a black suit. It looked oddly like the man she saw as a little girl. She later found out it was her great-grandfather, who had lived down the road and built the house where she saw the ghost. He had died before she was born.

"That was my first ghost experience," she said.

Because of that, she admits ghosts and phantoms tend not to scare her. And when her daughter sees a possible ghost on the side of the railroad tracks?

"I wasn't scared, just kind of surprised," she said.

The Spook House

Bill Tomkins wondered about the old, white house when he moved to Frank Street in Laurens County in the mid-1990s. It appeared to be what was left of an antebellum plantation. The two-story home had an old, rickety picket fence and a black roof. A couple of small buildings surrounded it, and several giant maple trees loomed over its side. He figured the building must be abandoned, based on the condition and the fact that he never saw anyone going in or out.

But a few nights after moving into his home down the road, he noticed some lights on inside. Well, he thought to himself, maybe someone did live inside the old home. Over the next few weeks he continued to drive by the old place—never seeing anyone inside, but always seeing the lights on. The windows were usually drawn, so he could never see if anyone was moving about. It was definitely well lit, not someone inside with a candle or small fire.

He finally asked another neighbor who lived in the old mansion. The neighbor just smiled and replied, "Oh, you know, ghosts." Tomkins thought his neighbor was kidding, but the serious look on the old man's face made him shiver.

"The guy told me for as long as he could remember, there would be lights on inside that home even though there were no lamps and no electricity running to the home," Tomkins recalled.

So who were the ghosts in real life and why do they still haunt the old place, which is often called The Spook House?

"The feeling around here is they don't bother us, so we won't bother them," Tomkins said.

The Open Windows

This is a story where the teller didn't want to be named, nor the name of the ghost to be mentioned. The ghost's name is fairly prominent and the woman's home is also well known. But the story was too good to leave out.

When the woman and her husband moved into the home, they started some minor renovations. They believe this is what sparked the ghost's interest, which focused on a particular pair of upstairs windows.

The woman said it all started in early autumn, when she closed the windows to keep out the cold. She came back the next day and noticed they were open. So, she and her husband decided to close them together and make sure the latches were tight, but the next day the windows were open again. They figured there might be a problem with the hinges, so they hired a handyman to come and look at the windows. He screwed them shut.

The next day, though, the couple went upstairs to check the windows. Again, they were open and the screws were lying on the floor. The woman was fed up. Since no one else had been in the house, she figured it was the ghost of a previous owner. She called out the man's name to stop opening the windows because it was getting cold all the time. Just as she did this, a stack of books against the wall came crashing down.

Our heroine mentioned the story to one of the previous owners' children, by then a grown man. The son replied that it was not his father. Rather, his mother was likely the entity opening the windows because she always kept them open.

With that in mind, the woman locked the windows a fourth time and nailed them shut. As she did it, she called out to the ghost by name to say what she was doing. The lights turned off, but the woman was able to turn them back on. More importantly, the windows in the room never mysteriously opened by themselves again.

A Legend Put to Rest

Patrick Wilson has been hearing for years that the Greenville hotel he runs, the Embassy Suites & Inn on Verdae Boulevard, is haunted by the ghost of a worker who died during construction. One legend states doors and windows open and close on their own. Another holds that random lights at the hotel, which overlooks a gorgeous golf course, could be seen on when the hotel was under construction and supposed to be without power.

Wilson acknowledges the tragic death of the construction worker, but he can explain the story about the lights. People who say the lights weren't supposed to be on don't realize something. The hotel had full power during the time of the alleged "ghost lights." He chalks up stories of doors and windows to overactive imaginations. The hotel did host a small paranormal convention in 2003, which likely only added fuel to the ghost tale fires.

"It's funny because I hear these stories all the time," he said with a laugh. "They aren't true."

The Ghost in the Back Row

It was late and Allen and Suzanne McCalla were struggling to finish the set for the production of the Greenville Little Theatre's *A Flea in Her Ear*. As they banged on the props standing on the wooden stage, they got the strange feeling they were being watched. It was around 11 P.M. and they were supposed to be the only people inside the building.

It was very shadowy, so they couldn't see who was sitting there, but both believed it was a man. Suzanne kind of nudged her head toward Allen to go investigate. They thought a bum or someone had idled his way off the street. But as Allen walked up the ramp that is the center aisle, the man just vanished.

The McCallas aren't the only ones who have seen or heard strange things inside the two-story building over the years. The building is part of Heritage Green, which at one time was the home of the Greenville Woman's College. A Civil War–era hospital also once sat on the spot. The theater itself was built in 1967 as part of Greenville's efforts to refurbish that section of downtown. An art museum and the main county library followed within a few years. There are plans to add a regional history museum and a children's museum, and to renovate an existing building to house part of the Bob Jones University art collection on Heritage Green.

And while legends abound about the library, the Little Theatre is the place with the most ghost stories. Allen McCalla, who is the director, has been told the building is the most haunted in Greenville, but he doesn't believe it. Then again, he has heard some strange tales.

In 1990, one of the performers was on stage during a show. She claims she saw a woman wearing an 1860s-style dress walk onto the stage, cut across the actors, and then walk back off stage and vanish into the crowd. No one else saw the mysterious visitor. The ghost woman would later gain the name "Nancy," but McCalla said he didn't know where that name came from.

"People still come in all the time and ask if Nancy has been seen lately," he said.

McCalla and others have said they have heard the large glass doors in the building's rear open and close, but no one ever comes in. The doors are rather heavy and can't be pushed by the wind. Someone has to open and shut them to get through. There is no explanation for what makes that noise.

Two Lancaster Tales

Gregory Graveyard is an old cemetery from the late 1600s or the early 1700s. Some claim the sounds of children laughing and playing can be heard coming from there even when no one can be seen. But who says ghosts need to be seen to be heard? Some report you can also hear a preacher saying a small prayer over a grave. The graveyard is located on Highway 903, heading away from Lancaster city limits.

There is also the story of the Devil's Stomping Ground, which is located near Highway 521. The story has nothing to do with the same-named ghost area in North Carolina, but is interesting in its own right. It involves a forty-foot circular area that is devoid of any vegetation. The legend states the Waxhaw and Catawba tribes used the spot for executions. Evil spirits were said to frequently visit the site to collect the condemned souls of the executed, and that is why nothing grows there.

A second legend is that the Devil would come to the spot to ponder ways of being evil. Either way, people visiting the site report an overwhelming feeling of dread, despair, and nausea when standing in the circle. People also claim that if you put objects in the circle, such as sticks or rocks, by the next morning they will be gone or moved outside of the circle.